A
W-14/5

HEAVEN HAS CLAWS

TRYING TO HOIST OUR COVERS

ADRIAN CONAN DOYLE

★

HEAVEN
HAS CLAWS

★

LONDON
JOHN MURRAY, ALBEMARLE STREET, W

FIRST EDITION 1952

Text printed in Holland by Vonk & Co's Drukkery, Zeist
Illustrations printed by Latimer Trend & Co., Ltd. Plymouth,
Bound by G. & J. Kitcat, Ltd. London
and
Published by John Murray (Publishers) Ltd.

TO THE OTHER WILD DUCK I DEDICATE THIS BOOK.

ACKNOWLEDGMENTS

I wish to record my grateful thanks for the encouragement and in some cases invaluable assistance which I received during the course of my Expedition; to H. H. The Sultan of Zanzibar; Mr. Jack Sinclair, C.M.G., O.B.E.; Commander Milner, R.N.; Mr. Edward Rodwell of *The Mombasa Times;* Mr. H. W. Austin and Capt. Bill Byles, both of the Union Castle Line; Mr. Dmitri Lupis; Mr. Arnold Klosser of the Inkosana and Major Grundy of the Huria. My especial thanks are due to my secretary, Mr. Corneille Benoist, for his marvellous skill in deciphering a manuscript richly steeped in spilt tea, candle wax and salt water. Finally, I raise my glass to a brave old man who, in the bosom of his ancient race, now awaits the call of Allah — to Ali Mahommet Ghilani, gentleman and dhow captain.

CONTENTS

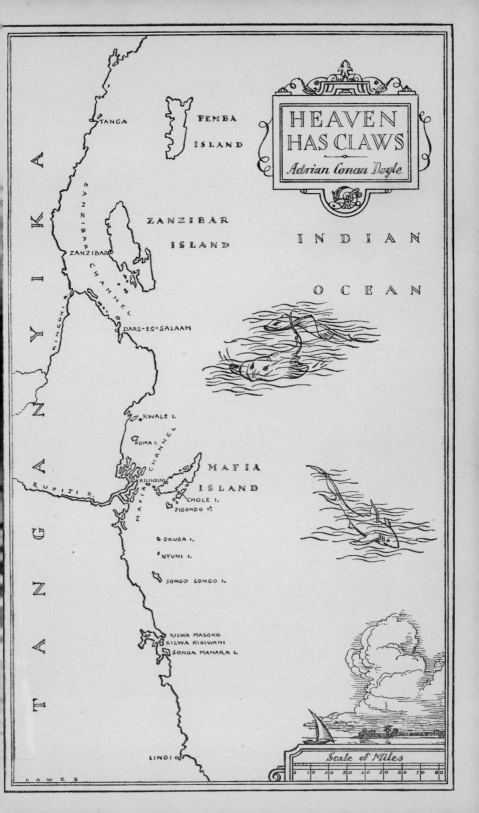

HEAVEN
HAS CLAWS

Adrian Conan Doyle

TANGA

PEMBA
ISLAND

ZANZIBAR

ZANZIBAR
ISLAND

ZANZIBAR CHANNEL

ZANZIBAR

DARS-ES-SALAAM

INDIAN

OCEAN

T A N G A N Y I K A

RINGONI R.

KWALE I.

KOMA I.

RUFIJI R.

KILINDINI

MAFIA CHANNEL

MAFIA
ISLAND

CHOLE I.
JIBONDO I.

OKUSA I.

NYUNI I.

SONGO SONGO I.

KILWA MASOKO
KILWA KISIWANI
SONGA MANARA I.

LINDI

H. A. W. E. S.

Scale of Miles

0 10 20 30 40 50 60 70 80

ILLUSTRATIONS

"Yet vagabondage means escape from slavery and the life of the roads means liberty.

To take the decision, to cast off all the bonds with which modern life and the weakness of our own hearts have charged us, to arm ourselves with the symbolic sack and staff of the pilgrim and *to depart* . . ."

ISABELLA EBERHARDT.

CHAPTER 1

CITADEL OF FREEDOM

I t was my brother Denis who first proposed that my wife and I should take up our residence in Tangier. He had known the town some years previously in the sunset of its charm, and unaware of the fundamental changes that had taken place, he advised us to give it a trial. For a year Anna and I, to say nothing of the bulldog, had been wandering about Europe, through France, Switzerland, Italy and even the Juliano-haunted mountains of Sicily in a hopeless search for sanity and freedom, and by the time that we reached the coast of Morocco we were already prepossessed in favour of any city or zone that was said to be both free and non-political. Nor were we disappointed so far as the old Arab portion of Tangier is concerned.

From the Petit Socco, a dirty little square lined with garish cafés and paraded nocturnally by contrabandists, prostitutes, pimps, polyglots and tourists, a maze of narrow tortuous streets, shadowy and mysterious, wind in a gentle ascent towards the Kasbah and its thousand years' old ramparts. Here, indeed, are the frowning bastions of the Barbary Coast reeking with their memories of treachery, intrigue and the sheen of steel; of slaves and slavers and slim pirate galleys. Three hundred feet above the surf, the cold grace of the archway in the outer rampart is a door of remembrance poised between the stars and the sea, and on moonlight nights the elusiveness of dreams steals over the face of this ancient town. The tiny streets are mere shadows between walls of pale blue ice. Daturas, those lovely white blossoms from which the Arab

women distil their stealthy poisons, hang like great teardrops against a background of moonwashed masonry and dark star-entangled arches leading into little gardens drowsy with the perfume of sleeping flowers and the clean aroma of the gum trees that have changed into pillars of silver with the rising of the moon. In the streets the hooded shapes of men and the veiled women, moving with that marvellous sexual grace that is a lost art to their emancipated sisters, are completely in keeping with this ageless stage on which they pass their destiny, and their reactions and emotions, the very essence of their lives, remain unchanged beneath all the charges and trumpet calls of History. Among the throngs that jostle and push through the twisting alleys, one notices a high proportion of creamy-skinned beauty in the Arab women whose eyes, eloquently lovely above their yashmaks, possess a velvet quality which one can only describe as the glance of a sensual gazelle. Incidentally, has woman ever discovered a more devastatingly effective weapon than the yashmak, that mist of flimsy chiffon and gold damaskwork which imbues her faintly veiled features with an elfin beauty and would change the eyes of a Lady Mayoress into twin pools of magic and forbidden delight. The Paris fashion-house that ventures to introduce a yashmak for evening wear should meet with success, for it is kind both to the beautiful and the less beautiful.

The old Arab town occupies roughly a half of Tangier and marks an abrupt line against the sprawling modern city beyond which, at a distance of four miles, rise two hills; the Old Mountain and the New. It was on the latter that at long last, full of hope and anticipation, we settled into a house that had been built some eighty years previously by the family of Sir John Drummond-Hay, one of the great pioneers of British interests in Morocco. All our effects had arrived by ship from England

and for a month we lived in an exciting whirl of furniture to be arranged, pictures to be hung, armour to be cleaned and all the hundred and one details that characterise the planting of roots, until at last, with everything accomplished, we settled down to the presumed peace and enjoyment of life in the famous International Zone.

On the Mountain, high above the white city, we came to know the friendship of many charming people, mostly elderly and addicted to those old-fashioned values that alone give us the right to classify ourselves above the shellfish. We found it a life of good neighbourliness and of those simple forms of kindness and honour and decency that, in distinguishing the contact of all men one with the other, represents both the necessity for, and the justification of, Freedom. If Tangier began and ended with the old Arab town and the old-fashioned European people on the Mountain, then the facts that the electric lights are given to failure, the water supply deficient, and the meat so tough that it is like unto chewing an ancient breastplate, are mere details that would count not at all against the infinite privilege of living in that state of liberty which has come to mean more to man, suffocating in his selfmade shroud, than the wealth of Eldorado.

But it is a very different story in the white town, sprawling between the Mountain and the Arab citadel. This is the *real* Tangier, the forced growth of war and restriction and misery in the outside world. To bring into correct focus this stronghold of Freedom, a state free of income tax, free of rates, free in its international currency, free of political parties, equality of nationalism, it is essential that one should appreciate that there are in effect two populations, one literally imposed or grafted on the other. The majority of citizens born and bred in Tangier are decent, honest, kindly and hard-working people and full of civic pride in the ancient history of their land and ancestry. The holocaust of war, bringing in its wake the ruin of nameless millions coupled with international financal restrictions, changed Tangier, as it were overnight, from a pleasant sleepy town of pleasant easy-going people into ideologically the most important place in the world, the last Free City. Every citizen whose country had signed the Algeciras Treaty of 1924 had the right to enter. By hook or crook displaced persons swarmed in their thousand through the loop-holes of the entry regulations, and thus, while the gun muzzles of Europe were still hot to the touch, the stream of human wanderers was already settling on the last citadel of liberty. Many of these people were decent and respectable folk carrying within themselves the attributes of good citizenship. But, like the gin pedlars who follow on the heels of the pioneers of a new continent, there commenced a deadly infiltration of racketeers, blackguards and financial pimps from the dowdy cafés of war-shattered Europe, creamed and spiced with a litter of needy adventurers, some of excellent family, who emerging from the great capitals and the Balkans slithered into Tangier on fortune bent. It is the machinations of these elements and not the honest majority of hard-working officials, residents and citizens, who have made the name of Tangier a hissing and a by-word. The whisper of evil is much more satisfying to the eardrum of the world than all the clarions of virtue.

It was not long before we were 'discovered' by the ever-alert financial pushers, and, regularly and uninvited, gentlemen began to intrude into our house with no other object in mind apparently than the purely altruistic one of making me a millionaire within a matter of months. I fear that they found me unco-operative as I preferred to remain among the more exclusive circle of non-millionaires. By good fortune rather than judgment, in the main we avoided the traps of the swindlers but whenever we afforded financial assistance and hospitality to those who came to us in apparently genuine stress we were robbed and filched until, once convinced that the coffers and the larder were finally closed against them, the oft-befriended had to content themselves with calumny, complaint and slander, subject only to the necessary proviso that they should be beyond reach of my riding crop. One young Czech who had received every benefit decided at last that we oldfashioned and unbusinesslike gentlemen should know him for the bold spirit that he was and consequently spat in a lady's face in a public restaurant; while a Balkan compatriot, a man of excellent family, showed an almost laudable restraint in limiting himself to the abstraction of my gold cigarette holder, presumably as the price of the pleasure of his company at dinner. The wide zoological variety of social and financial climbers whose descent on Tangier has caused much discomfort to the Administration and even more to the private resident, can be seen in even the tiniest of vignettes, though for decency's sake it is necessary that we should clothe them in so perfect a disguise that each individual may be certain to recognise himself only through the response of his own conscience or intellect. On second thoughts, neither word is applicable.

Here we have, shall we call him a South-American, a perfect model for one of Rubens's gross peasants, launched into life from a background of tinned vegetables and equipped with a wife nibbled to death with social ambitions. Despite the fact that their door falls off its hinges before anything that possesses a title, real or false, and falls not in vain owing to the free drinks that lurk within, they remain where they began; two figures on a gilded tomato can. There is the gentleman who stole a bank, lock, stock and barrel, surely a unique performance that presumably justifies his presence at official soirées and gives him some degree of good natured rivalry with the more conventional financier whose patriarchal whiskers are doubtless worn to disguise him from the donkeys whose rectums, well packed with smuggled gold, launched him in his career. There, striding towards the police station wherein a frank-faced English youth is busily explaining that he did not murder his rival in contraband and hi-jack his boat, is the stately figure of one of our leading doctors, doubtless musing on those good old days when he was employed professionally in one of Hitler's concentration camps. And now comes a silver voice, flitting from bar to bar, before whom we must stand abashed, for what counts pedigree and coat armour in the presence of one who claims intimacy with "the dear Queen" and every other Royal personage for the past two hundred years. She assures us that she has been courted, chased, hopelessly compromised by every nobleman above the rank of marquis, that she is "of", and believing her implicitly we worry over the fact that she has the words "kitchen wench" in oil paint on her forehead. On the Place de France are three tall fellows talking together in a statuesque group; the figure on the right is that of a polished gentleman who hires out his polished motorcar complete with his polished mistress for polished coin; the sleek but ill-bred Spaniard on the left, exploring his jaws with a toothpick, is a professional sponger with a side line in perjury, while the third man, his father, a banana pedlar from Hann, has arrived to accommodate his son's police record and to assist him in avoiding his debts. They stand with the rigidity of telephone poles until the dropping of a peseta on the pavement converts them as if by magic into eager hairpins.

In their periodic attacks on this town, British and American writers and journalists have completely missed the real essence of its sordidness. They concentrate upon the contrabandists and smugglers but in actual fact many of these toughs are superior animals to the cadgers and climbers glittering with dubious titles who clutter up the bars of the Place de France, and the financial adventurers who, too often under the guise of business men, have settled in Tangier and thriven most mightily by victimising the decent majority.

However our experiences were no worse and no better than those of others and merely served to teach us that which so many wiser heads than ours had already learned, namely: that dishonour and ingratitude are synonymous with the flow of displaced humanity.

Whenever corruption plays a large part in the life of a town or country there is to be seen an unmistakable reflection throughout the whole design of moral issues. Tangier is no exception to the rule. In the sand pits stagger dreadful scarecrow horses, their starved bodies galled with harness sores, open wounds the size of a man's hand, and the two rascally Spaniards who own these trains of walking death, are quite prepared to face the paltry fines to which they are liable, so long as the demand for bricks makes it worth their while to carry the wet sand from the shore to the distant roadway. In the streets the living poultry are carried by their feet in bundles, their heads hanging and sometimes trailing on the ground. This year saw the opening of pigeon shooting for the local "sportsmen", God save the mark! Ten thousand birds were brought from Spain and, released from dark boxes, their wing and tail feathers having been partly torn out, the wretched creatures were given not a chance. Guns roared, countless birds perished and even more were left wounded and strug-

2

gling upon the ground. The coup de grâce, demanded in any civilized country, would have cost effort and therefore it was easier to throw the wounded birds into the same boxes as the dead ones. Large silver trophies were presented by the Administration to the heroes of the day; there was much suburban representation which afforded the little ladies a chance to show off the limitations of their wardrobes; and then all departed back to town smelling faintly of cordite, brilliantine and spilt blood. In the face of complete official apathy, the cause of the animals is waged by one brave tired man, Mr. Quarrington, chief of the Sick Animals' Dispensary, and solidly with him stand the nucleus of decent people of all ages and nationalities. It is high time that the attention of the animal lovers of the world was turned to the pretty town that shimmers and smirks on the great lunar arch of the bay between Spartel and Malabata.

In despite of all, in our house on the Mountain we were well aware of the advantages that belonged to our life in this locality. The price of living was well below that of other countries, servants were plentiful and income tax as such did not exist. From time to time the rather jumbled pattern of existence was enlivened by saturnine incidents such as the occasion when a Spanish woman carrying a monkey in the Petit Socco struck an Arab cake vendor who immediately struck the monkey, was in turn hit by a Spanish policemen who was hit in his turn by an Arab policeman, the whole ending in a free-for-all in which everybody who could claim a Spaniard or an Arab in the family tree joined most heartily. Then, again, there was the festive moment when a ship bound for the Near East with a huge cargo of rubber goods, dumped the lot on Tangier docks. Some meddler opened the cases and the local Trade Winds handsomely accomplished the rest. For days the lower part of the town was ankle-deep in strange objects, some brilliantly coloured; one's car ran silently on rubber-covered streets, and rude boys idled away the hours by inflating the erstwhile merchandise into long thin balloons.

Variety ranging from the ludicrous to the murderous is the great compensating factor of Tangier life, and the monthly quota of disappearances, reappearances, falsehoods, suspected truths, chicanery and sudden flashes of individual kindness and generosity would justify a permanent chronicler working day and night to produce a book which, though strictly confined to true incidents interwoven in a pattern of rumour, would be immediately discredited by the rest of the world.

But what of our own future? Nearly two years had passed since our arrival in Morocco and now, looking down from our terrace upon the twinkling lights of the town, Anna and I discussed the situation. We had sampled the lunacy of a once free nation that had become a controlled state and in consequence sold our home. Our sojourn in the free zone of Tangier had taught us in return that freedom misused has no more to offer than the "New" Europe with its Picasso-riddled mind and its soul spattered with blood and hot metal.

What did we want from life? Could we in practice place adventure and freedom before comfort and luxury? We were no longer so young and the material things that surrounded us, the very relics of our forbears, had come to be the casket of our lives.

"We've talked often enough about the futility of modern life," I said to Anna. "Do you really think that you could stand up to the physical hardship of spending the remaining years of our youth in pursuit of real adventure among the forgotten or the unexplored places of the world? You've had a sample of it already on a mild scale when you were with me in the Cameroons before the war."

"I'm as sick of it all as you are," she replied. "I will go any-
where with you but on one condition."

"And that is?"

She twisted the ear of the huge bulldog sitting beside her on
the swing seat.

"Jum-Jum must go too," she smiled.

CHAPTER 2

A CHANGING WORLD

Six months passed, and there had been much to do in the time. Mr. F. A. Mitchell-Hedges, the well-known big game fisherman and explorer who had accomplished such fine work among the Maya ruins of Central America, had been a near neighbour of ours in the New Forest. I knew that the old wanderlust was moving within him and so, once we had decided definitely to leave civilization, I wrote to him and informed him of our views. His reaction was immediate. Let us merge forces. But for what destination? By one of those curious coincidences which are more common in life than our novelists would have us believe, we exchanged identical suggestions on the subject. M. H. had fished the Caribbean reefs and parts of the Pacific. I had fished North African waters and the South Atlantic. During a recent visit to South Africa he had encountered a man who had just returned with his trading schooner from a long sea voyage that had taken him among the Amirantes and Aldebras, groups of coral islands that formed an outflung portion of the Seychelles, and he had spoken of gigantic shark and Manta ray the size of carpets rising from the surface of the sea. In Tangier, five thousand miles away I had made a careful note of these very islands, owing to a statement contained in Van Campen Heilner's book apropos vague rumours of huge fish among the lesser known islands of the Indian Ocean. Amirantes, wrote Mitchel-Hedges; Amirantes, wrote I; and our letters crossed. Now, came the period of preparation. Fortunately I had a great deal of gear all ready to hand, for Anna and I had been on the point of embarking on a five years' expedition to the Pacific in 1939. Nevertheless there was an enormous amount to be done, and it is largely thanks to the efficiency of my friend and secretary, Mr. Corneille Benoist, that everything was accomplished in time. Together, we engaged in a seemingly endless correspondence with American line and rod and reel makers; with steamship companies and makers of harpoons and people who dealt in powerful wire traces and manila ropes that might or might not be capable of resisting the awful charge of the monsters of the deep. From Norway came two cwt. of huge steel hooks, each measuring more than a foot in length. Slowly the stuff mounted up until the basement of our house took on the appearance of a cross between a gunsmith's and a ships' chandler's yard. From time to time frenzied letters from Mitchell-Hedges would inform us that his house was in the same state. No detail must be overlooked. We must be self-sufficient for every necessity of life save for fish, turtle-meat and the milk of coconuts. Time flew by.

The final few days were a whirl of packing and checking and listing, culminating in a last romantic night spent in wandering in the moonlight along the ancient Kasbah battlements high above the sea. A few hours later, while the purple shadows still hung upon the valley and the distant mountain peaks were black against the pale saffron glow of the dawn, our faithful Arab servants had gathered to wish us farewell, all the paraphernalia, including the bulldog, loaded, and we had turned to take a last look at the kindly house, now rose pink in the early light, that contained all the material things that we loved best in the world. We had tried the new civilization minus the old values of our ancestors and we knew it for what it is. We had tried the Free Zone and knew it for something little better. Please God that in the wild places of the earth, in tune with the vast pageantry of creation we might find some place untouched by the spiritual and mental frustration of modern life.

In company with Mr. Benoist and Jean Ramsden, a young Marine attached to the American Legation and incidentally a very promising archaeologist, we crossed to Gibraltar from whence we were to sail in the *Dunnottar Castle* for Mombasa. Mitchell-Hedges, accompanied by his daughter, would be on the ship, complete with gear. My friend Mr. Tamplin, the Marine Superintendent of Gibraltar, was on the quay to greet us and the sight of his strong, stalwart figure was the very tonic that we needed to raise our spirits. However beneficial the reason, the roots of teeth are not the only ones that hurt when pulled. With his usual kindness Tamplin had arranged everything for us and had even contrived to surmount the blackmailing practices of the Gibraltese Spanish porters who are in the habit of forcing travellers to agree to exorbitant fees before they will handle a piece of luggage.

I have always liked Gibraltar. Dull it may be, yet there is something definite and purposeful about the place, and after dark there is more than a touch of old Italy in the grey silent squares and shuttered houses of the sleeping Rock. At eleven o'clock that night we received disturbing news. A passenger on the *Dunnottar Castle* had gone down with Polio and had been duly taken off at Gravesend. Since then, three more passengers had been segregated as a precautionary measure and were to be landed under medical supervision when the ship arrived at Gibraltar in the morning. It rested now in the hands of the medical authorities whether or not the whole ship should be placed in quarantine, in which case we should not be permitted to board her. However, at six a.m. the medicos having decided at last that the vessel be allowed to enter and leave the port after the removal of the segregated passengers, we went aboard and, with the hurly-burly over and under way at last, we settled down to the lazy beat of shipboard life.

The weather was blue silk, the Mediterranean like a tropic sea. Marseilles, with French life progressing well; then Genoa, with Italian life progressing even better. It is a pity that the tax payer and voter cannot treat the whole British Government to a forced march around the Continent accompanied by a ruthless and enclosing ring of long-suffering British housewives. Indeed, if only some newspaper would find the courage to publish the priced menus of the ordinary Continental restaurants! Lose a war and you get the chicken. Win it and you get the whalemeat. Sometimes one is tempted to wonder if we have not created a lunatic world.

A few nights later we were on the bridge, gazing through the darkness at a distant ruddy spark that hung in the sky, glowering and sullen as an angry star. However often one passes Stromboli, the wicked old volcano has the same fascination. As we approached across a sea of black glass a livid pall of gases shone on the clouds above the crater. And then, as though a trap door from the infernal regions had been flung wide, a fountain of flame and white hot lava shot into the night sky to fall away in glowing driblets among the ravines and crevices. Again and again the serrated peak shone with a pulsing hell light while the air above the mountain flared and shimmered, as with the play of red lightning. The impressiveness of the whole scene was greatly emphasised by the silence enwrapping it. One could hear a fish jumping on the surface of the sea. The power of man to become inured to danger is nowhere better illustrated than among those hardy souls who dwell amidst the rich vineyards flourishing on the

- 24 -

lower slopes of the volcano. Truly do they squeeze their grapes in the palm of death's hand.

With memories of pre-war Port Said I had warned Anna that none of her blandishments would persuade me to add one of the great ostrich feather fans to our mountain of baggage. I could have saved my breath, for Port Said had moved with the times. The Bum-boat men littered the decks with revolting heaps of brief cases, Birmingham shirts, socks and gimcrack necklaces. Gone were the glorious fans of white and black ostrich plumes, the sprays of egret feathers, the little cups shimmering to the brim with unset moonstones and the white grin of the shark jaws. Of the old way of life there now remained nothing save one careworn gentleman outside the dock gates peddling intimate postcards of Port Said domesticity. Alas, for "…the glory that was Greece, And the grandeur that was Rome."

August, the Red Sea and heat unbelievable. The great arch of the horizon shimmered with the hues of a peacock's tail and the sun was mighty in his glory. Between sea and sky a hazy deathliness showed where the lands of the Old Testament fried in their sand. At last we were entering big-fish waters and my thoughts turned eagerly to a problem which lay at the root of this expedition and which has interested the human imagination from the beginning.

Does the sea still preserve its mysteries? Do there still exist in the depths of the ocean forms of life, perhaps monsters of life, as yet unknown to Science? As a field zoologist and fisherman, I had held definite views on this question for twenty years past. The circumstantial evidence pronounced very strongly in the affirmative. I had yet to meet the experienced big game fisherman — and these are the very men who do not confuse giant squids or gas-blown whales with Plesiosaurii — or the sea-going icthyologist who did not hold similar views. I had yet to meet the armchair Zoologist who did not deride them. And then, in 1938, had come the South African bombshell, that electrifying drama which left the sceptics gaping. A trawling net operating in the Indian Ocean, off East London, brought to the surface a most curious creature, repulsive yet beautiful. It was a fish, some five feet in length, its head undershot and gap-toothed, its body covered not with scales but with enamelled plates of a lovely translucent blue. Rushed to Grahamstown University, it was instantly recognised by the astounded scientists as nothing less than a Ganoid, a type of fish believed to have been extinct since the period of the Red Sandstone, more than sixty million years ago. Compared with this creature, the great sea-saurians were things of yesterday! To top it all, just three weeks later a similar specimen, but dead, was washed up on the shore. Little wonder that the wires of the world were hot with news of a great discovery in the light of which it is now more necessary than ever for cautious yet open-minded men to reconsider the evidence of unknown monsters that, reported from all the oceans of the globe, in the past have been too lightly cast aside. Who knows what may dwell in the Tuscarora Deep, those eight miles sheer of midnight waters, or in the vast expanses of any of our seas, so tenuously traversed by narrow shipping lanes?

Mitchell-Hedges in his researches among the Bay Islands of the Caribbean had brought to light no less than twenty-five hitherto unknown species of fish. Fine work, indeed. And to what size do known species run? My companion held the view that he had never caught a big fish despite the fact that his thirty-one foot Pacific Sawfish weighed 5'700 lbs. I think that he is right. For what is a big fish? To that we shall know the answer only when the waters have gone from the depths of the sea. In the meantime, the primary object of our expedition was to come to close grips with the sea life, known or unknown, and we were fully prepared to face all risks and discomforts with that goal in mind.

Outwardly, Port Sudan appeared little changed. Here was the same dust and display of shells and corals stained to various hues by the use of coloured ink, and, above all, the Fuzzie-Wuzzies with their heads of golly-wog hair and their swaggering savagery. They are among the finest fighting races in the world, and they know it. On the heat-shimmering dock they squatted in their lines awaiting the opening of the hatches while their leader, a fellow with a dirty red turban around his head and the eye of a goshawk, sprawled on a throne of oildrums.

I ran out a shark line baited with half a pig's head and hoped for the best, and as we watched the pale green glimmer of the bait far down in the water the man beside me told of a nasty incident that he had witnessed a few voyages previously at this very dock. A native boy diving for pennies came to the surface minus one leg and, on being quickly hauled on to a lighter, the poor lad had died immediately. With this story in my ears it would have been a great satisfaction to have rid the Port of one of its sea-tigers but the Gods decreed otherwise.

That day the temperature was 116° in the shade and 142° in the sun. Sleep was impossible. And towards midnight we took our rods and in an Arab boat trolled in the direction of the harbour mouth. The full moon, turning the bay into a great sheet of silver, illumined even the depths of the sea with a phantom radiance and, far below the keel of the boat, rounded lumps of coral shone palely like the skulls of lost mariners. I had a strike and with virtually no fight reeled in a Garfish. It was about two feet in length with an eel-shaped body and long thin forceps jaws. A few minutes later the same performance was repeated. By now we were near the mouth of the harbour, and the noise was astounding. It was as though we were surrounded by water fowl, their wings beating the surface with the rush of the take-off. Crash, splash, flurry, splash! They were in fact big fish, Cavalli Jack and Albacore, feeding on the swarming schools of fry. Then, three times in quick succession, I was broken up, in each case the wire traces that fasten the hook to the line being bitten clean through. These were worthy opponents, indeed. At two a.m. everything was silent, not a strike, not a ripple and, tired but content, we turned our oars towards the distant lights of the ship.

Early next morning a school of very large Cavalli Jack appeared close alongside, hunting for breakfast, and one could clearly follow the movements of their silver bodies, crescent shaped tails and brilliant yellow fins. Their leader was an absolute giant that M. H. and I both reckoned to be at least 30 lbs. heavier than the present world record of 88 lbs. Hedges had caught a 94 pounder in the Caribbean but on a thicker line than is permitted for that classification of fish, and he judged the beauty in the water below at a good 120 lbs. A steward threw over a lump of fish attached to a line as thick as a clothes' rope. The Cavalli struck, tore off sixty yards and then burst the line like a piece of cotton.

The behaviour of this same giant five minutes later went to confirm my views that fish, in contrast to all, warmblooded creatures, are virtually impervious to pain. Though they react strongly to the instinctive consciousness that they have been touched, that there is an inexplicable interference with their movements, there is strong evidence that pain as such plays little part in the nerve centres of a fish. An excellent example

- 28 -

of this can be seen in the reports of whalers who, in their attempts to preserve the body of a dead whale, have slashed at attacking sharks with their razor-sharp blubber spades, cutting off fins, tails and great lumps of flesh, yet in spite of the infliction of these mutilations the sharks have continued to snap and tear and gorge themselves on the whale until they themselves have turned belly upwards, dead through loss of blood!

In this instance, as I cut away the half pig's head from the shark hook and threw it into the water, the great Cavalli came up with a rush, seized the meat in its recently wounded jaws and shaking it to and fro like a savage bulldog, vanished into the depths. If destiny permit, I must return to the Red Sea, for there is mighty medicine to be made in its waters.

Aden; the Straits of Bab-el-Mandib, and at last our sea of adventure, the Indian Ocean, all white-capped with the northeast monsoon.

That night, the coast of Italian Somaliland faintly visible through the darkness, I smoked my pipe and listened to a strange story. The teller was a man who had spent the past six years after big game in the lesser known parts of Africa and is in line for a "Game Wardenship" in the hinterland. I was already aware of his reputation as a taxidermist, for the Regents Park Zoo had entrusted him on two occasions calling for the utmost skill in preserving freak specimens, and his practical experience in the field of African game covered such rarities as the Bongo, the Okapi and the Greater Koodoo. We discussed the strange legends of the Nandi Bear and the Great Lau.

"During your safaris in Africa, did you ever encounter the Unknown?" I asked.

"Well, yes, as it happens I did," he replied.

And I will let him tell the story in his own words.

"I was on safari along a very remote part of the Sudan-

Abyssinian border, and late one afternoon I came upon a queer kind of place. The landscape is pretty arid and burnt up in those parts and I suppose that there must have been a perpetual underground spring or something of that sort to account for the outcrop of trees and vivid green swamp covered with high rushes that filled a dip between two hills. My natives intimated that we should head off in another direction but I wanted a closer look. That greenery should spell water. On entering the belt of trees I slowed up and slipped the safety catch off my rifle for I had become suddenly aware that there was something moving ahead of me. A moment later I was gaping through the leaves at the most fantastic looking creature I ever saw in my life. The trees were literally a belt encircling an open space with a large ants' nest at one end. On the ground near the ants' nest but not feeding on it was a thing like a huge lizard. It was, I should say, from ten to twelve feet in length, a dirty grey in colour and with a saurian type head. The skin was curiously lumpy and right down the back and tail ran a high crest of wattles. I noticed the great claws gleaming on its feet as I raised my rifle. But I couldn 't shoot. I *knew* as I looked down the sights that I was in the presence of something incredibly rare; indeed I have neither seen nor heard of anything remotely like it! A few moments later it began to move, waddling away in the direction of the swamp, and as soon as its tail had vanished amid the rushes, I ran forward to examine the spoor. The marks were three-toed but very slurred which means that the Thing slithered its feet rather than paced. Then I sat down and drew it while the details were fresh in my mind. My boys were waiting for me outside the green belt and apparently knew something about the creature, for they gave it a native name and added an expression which it is impossible to translate literally. In effect, it means 'A bad 'un'! Well, when I got back to more civilized parts and told my friends there was a lot of amusement and loose talk about drinking. As it happens, the one thing that I don't do is to touch spirits when I'm on safari."

"I'd like to go with you to that place," I said at last.

"Well, I am hoping to go back one day," he replied, "and the next time I'll take a camera."

A few days later, with the green loom of Africa on every side, our anchor chains clanked down in Kilindini, the harbour of Mombasa, and the first stage of our journey had come to an end.

CHAPTER 3

"INDIAN EAST AFRICA"

I stood and gaped in the centre of Mombasa. Surely we must have taken the wrong turning somewhere on the voyage and arrived not in Africa but in India. Mombasa I well remembered twenty years ago as a place of a few hundred whites and many thousands of Africans. But this was certainly India. A large proportion of the higher and lower officials whom we had already encountered at the Port were Indian; eight shops out of every ten, Indian; most of the small cars and virtually all the big cars driven by Indians. The local schools were disgorging swarms of Indian children all over the streets. The air itself rustled with saris. My questioning and enquiries brought to light some most disconcerting information. There are twenty-five thousand Indians in the town against two thousand five hundred whites. In the case of every British subject entering this British Crown Colony there is a stiff examination in the shape of an interviewing officer and a lengthy immigration form; furthermore, where a British subject arriving for a job of work has to deposit £ 150 in cash, an Indian is called upon to deposit £ 10 only. Now, the East African government is composed of competent men, and presumably there is a reason for all this and it would be an impudence for a stranger to sit in judgment upon their running of this magnificent country, so criminally neglected in the way of practical help by successive British governments at home. Nevertheless there was a nasty reek in the atmosphere and it was neither the aroma of British beef nor East African game steak but of something more crafty and well-blooded with betel nut. What I saw in Gibraltar and in Mombasa and later in Zanzibar went to confirm my opinion that in the long run the greatest threat to our way of life will come not from the smoothheaded bestiality of Russia but from the infinitely more cunning Indian. Russia arouses the world to grasp the gun and sight the bomb; India moves in quietly with an ingratiating smile and a large bag of rupees. This state of affairs applies not merely to Mombasa and Nairobi but throughout every town and village of the interior, and those with an eye for fact are already addressing their letters to friends or relatives in "Mombasa, Indian East Africa" to the horror of the local post office. From all that I have seen of the changes that have occurred since my last visit in 1929, coupled with the views of those who have spent their lives in this part of the world, I have no hesitation in stating that unless the white authorities not only disclose the mailed fist but clench it around a spiked mace, within a decade East Africa will no longer form a part of the British Empire. It will be instead a dominion of an associated empire of India and Pakistan, and this enormous acquisition will take place as bloodlessly yet as completely and disastrously as, shall we say, the depredations of the white ant at work among the relics of Dr. Livingstone. And there are big men, *very* big men, behind the Indian movement, make no mistake about it.

In exploring Mombasa I was impressed by the civic growth of the community, the wide shady streets and particularly by the hospital which, standing on the tip of the Old Harbour headland, possesses certainly one of the finest medical sites in the world. The shops of the town, however, are filled with examples of bad handiwork and, worst of all, ivory. It is high time that the African authorities considered the question of the justification for the endless slaughter of that noble beast,

3

the bull elephant, for the sake of its tusks. In former days it was possible to justify the killing on the grounds that ivory was the medium for the exquisite art of the Chinese craftsman, but nowadays far the greater part of Africa's output of ivory goes to India and reappears as useless chunks of carving that are more in keeping with the skill of a schoolboy working in plasticine. It strikes one as absolutely unmoral that a bull elephant, probably two hundred years of age, should be duly slaughtered and the splendid tusks removed for no other purpose than to clutter up the market with a lot of rubbish worked in precious material but without any standard of craftsmanship whatsoever.

It was necessary for us to remain in Mombasa for a month as there was no boat for the Seychelles before the first week in October, and as it turned out the month's delay was to bring about a big change in our ultimate destination. In the meantime we made our headquarters at the lovely Nyali Beach Hotel, some five miles from the town and occupying a beautiful position on the edge of a lagoon girt by an outer reef separating the placid inner waters from the surf of the ocean proper.

One abortive day only did we spend in fishing when, sizzling in the heat, M.H. and I sat in an open boat in a channel that forms a break in the reef and fished and sweated and fried and blistered and had not so much as a strike while the other occupants of the boat, a mass of squids, sent a protesting stench to the pitiless sky. But the coping stone was awaiting our return. For, as we dragged ourselves wearily up the white coral beach we were accosted by a small boy.

"Have you been fishing? Have you caught anything?" he asked shrilly.

Our veracity being at stake, we answered no.

"You should have a net on the end of those," observed the

infant prodigy, pointing to our rods and then stumped off in search of some passing starfish.

The weeks had flown by and with the end of the month in sight we had to do some serious thinking. The Press of South Africa, in addition to the newspapers of East Africa, were featuring the plans of our expedition in columns and occasionally in headlines, and the question that had to be decided at once was whether or not our proposed destination was well chosen. During our sojourn many scraps and straws of information had come to hand. That there were great fish in the waters around the Seychelles was almost certain but the islets themselves were rather better known than I had imagined. Of ancient archaeological remains, there were none. South from Mombasa, however, far beyond Zanzibar, lay the Mafia Channel littered with coral isles and reputed to be the home of very large fish. Certainly no big game tackle had been brought to those waters; and beyond Mafia again lay the deep estuary of Kilwa Kisiwani with tales of undug ruins — rumour had it that some were founded in the days of the Queen of Sheba — now mouldering in the green twilight of the jungle. There were the Golden Isle, and Songa Manara with its virgin ruins. Songa Manara... the very name rang like a great harp! In any case, Seychelles or Kilwa, our work would be limited by the duration of the north-east monsoon. And at that point Fate, heavily disguised as a bulldog, waddled and panted on to the stage.

The only connection with the Seychelles lay with a British shipping company and we were now informed that, under a new regulation of the company, no dogs would be permitted on the ships. Jum-Jum had travelled without let or hindrance on many shipping lines and the introduction of this extraordinary regulation struck one as a most indefensible trespass upon the interests of passengers, bearing in mind that there was no alternative route to the Seychelles Islands. Upon further enquiry I was informed that this regulation had been recently introduced lest the presence of an animal, even so vile a creature as a dog, should offend the religious susceptibilities of any of the deck-cargo Indians; this despite the fact that the dog would be entirely segregate and travelling only as far as the Seychelles. I pointed out that the company had always carried passengers' pets in the past; why, then, the change? It was a new policy of the company, I was assured, to avoid all risks to the religious feelings of any Indian sect. I was deeply impressed. That a great shipping company should give religious susceptibility a priority over profit struck me as altogether magnificent. Had they not lost a great deal of money through the closing of the ship's bars, the existence of which would be an offence to the Mohammedans? What about the slowing of the ship through the fact that the crew stopped work on Sunday in accordance with Christian principles? Had they succeeded in finding a substitute for the removal of pork and bacon from the ship's menus in recognition of Jewish ethics? What was my surprise, however, in finding that none of these things apply.

The Kenya Veterinary authorities, having at first refused to believe in the existence of this by-law, informed me that it would lead eventually to serious trouble in view of the fact that no other shipping line served the fairly large white population of the Seychelles. I hope sincerely that it does. Anyway, the problem of our destination no longer existed. Anna and I cancelled our passages on the spot. Mitchell-Hedges, deciding to carry on with the Seychelles, duly departed complete with his gear and our good wishes for some record catches. And, from then on, things began to hum.

The spirit of co-operation and assistance that we received

on every side was simply magnificent. Mr. H. W. Austin, chief of the Union Castle Line's East African organisation, took it into his own able hands to smooth out the difficulties of manifests, storage of extra supplies of shark hooks from Norway, and all the myriad things that go to the launching of a human enterprise. At the offices of the *Mombasa Times* Mr. Edward Rodwell, the editor and author, placed at my disposal his own rich knowledge of Africa and its forgotten civilisations. At a moment of fearful crisis, when a weakness in the swivel fittings of our great lines had become apparent, the Royal Navy, in the shape of Commander Milner, R. N. stood by us and saved the situation. Incidentally, East Africa has good reason to be proud of the nucleus of the Royal East African Navy that has been brought into being by the efforts of Commander Milner. That one man, assisted by two other officers, can create out of a rocky point, some grass and a lot of African natives, the discipline, smartness and efficiency of a small-scale Greenwich within six months is nothing less than marvellous. But there it is.

Sixty-two boxes containing 10 tons of shark hooks, tinned food, ropes, wire traces, rods, reels, rifles, tools, cameras, ammunition and medicines heaped the wharfside, as we said au revoir to our kind friends at Mombasa and embarked on the trading schooner *The Southern Cross* en route to Zanzibar. A few hours later Kilindini had vanished over the horizon and night had fallen.

Sitting on a coil of rope in the stern of the little ship we watched the darkness, while above our heads the reeling stars seemed as near as the blobs of witch-flame glowing and tumbling in the trail of green fire that marked the ship's wake across the invisible waters. It was the hushed hour when a man asks himself whether he and his whole species are anything more than a comma in the Great Story. But the hour passes; the personal rises again in its normal perspective; and with it the time for a last pipe.

A dog had been the decisive factor. What lay ahead for Anna and me among the desolate isles of the Mafia Channel, in the bush land of Kilwa and on the waters of the Lazarus Bank, only Fate herself could know. And Fate is perhaps the only woman who keeps her secrets exclusively to herself.

CHAPTER 4

PYGMIES IN ROSE PETAL

The scent of cloves drifted over a peacock-coloured sea from the perfumed woods of Zanzibar. The great dhows from Muscat, high pooped and painted with bizarre designs along their counters swept in like a fleet of medieval galleons, their slanting lateen sails, snow-white against the brilliant blue of the sky, towering above the lines of dark figures that strained and panted over the sweep of each great oar. Mid a rolling of drums and crying of strange shrill trumpets, the stately ships bore down upon the end of their journey.

From Aden and the Gulf of Persia the dhows had come, as they had been coming unchanged in appearance and method since the days of Solomon; their sunken decks rubbed in shark oil and laden with cargoes of shark hide, copper ware and glorious chests filigreed and rivetted with brass work that shone in the sunlight like webs of gold. Traders on the outward run, beware the lonely fisherman in his outrigger canoe who encounters the homebound dhow, for in despite of the poetic names of their vessels — *News of God, Light of the Sea* and so forth, — these men are pirates when opportunity affords, and slaves fetch a higher price nowadays in the markets of Arabia than even bags of cloves or the creamy wealth of ivory. But, for all their sins, the men of the dhows are brave fellows in the face of the fearful risks inseparable from their 1400 miles tack across the Indian Ocean, and only last year no less than forty of these unwieldy ships were lost in a single typhoon.

Like the dhows, Zanzibar had remained virtually unchanged, and it was altogether wonderful to find ourselves again after a term of many years in a place that had resisted all the ugly opportunism of so-called modern development. Here were the old streets turning and twisting between dignified Arab houses whose doorways, richly carved and adorned with huge brass spikes, offered occasional glimpses of little gardens, all dreams and green shadow, beneath the sleepy droop of the palm trees. The white palace shone in the sun, the coffee vendors clanked their conical brass pots between bouts of serving passersby with real Mocha in tiny porcelain cups, and from beyond the groups of naked boys bathing in the marvellous clearness of the sea the crashing of the dhow cymbals and the thudding of their drums brought an echo from the ancient walls. The influence of the Sultan and the wise policy of former British Residents have combined to preserve the past in the present and, out-virtuing its poisoned memories as a clearing station of the slave trade, today Zanzibar drowses like a bowl of old rose petals on the green lap of Africa.

After making our way through a series of slits to our hotel we found good news awaiting us. For seven years past I had kept up a correspondence with Raymond Simmonds, the Australian war correspondent and journalist, and though we had never even seen each other a mutual goodwill had developed. In Australia he was a recognised expert on my father and his works and, in sharp contrast to many self-styled "experts" on the same subject in England, his articles on my father were drawn from no other sources than those of veracity and knowledge. Having journeyed to England where he visited my parents' resting place in the garden of Windlesham, he had flown on to Switzerland to see my brother and then to Tangier where he had missed me by nearly two months. Undismayed, Simmonds leapt into a plane for Abyssinia and the cable that awaited us in the hotel contained the news that he was journeying post haste to join the expedition for a short time before continuing on his journey to Australia. Two days later I was writing in my bedroom when the door opened and in came a short, powerfully built man. I stared at him blankly, noting the broad arch of the cranium above and the pugilist's jaw below.

"I'm Simmonds," he said faintly, mopping at his brow. "Beer, for the love of God!"

"You're very welcome on the expedition," I observed, after liquid refreshment had been rushed to the scene of action. "But you realise that we haven't the faintest idea of what is in store for us. We are no expert seamen, the waters around Mafia are a maze of coral reefs and we may not even return safely."

"In any case, I can be with you for a few weeks only," he replied. "As for the rest, I was in Hiroshima, and I reckon that I would prefer the moods of old Mother Nature whatever the risks."

After which, further comment would have been superfluous.

Shortly after our arrival, I was summoned to the palace for an Audience with His Highness the Sultan. In a pleasant study, hung with family portraits, armorial shields from British warships and all those personal little touches that make the difference between comfort and mere formality, I found a white-clad, white turbaned man with a grey beard and kindly intelligent eyes, combining in his majesty of presence that degree of gentle courtesy which is the hallmark of the man who is noble by nature as well as by birth. Over iced sherbet, we discussed the possibilities of great fish off the Zanzibar coast and the mystery of the ruined cities far to the South, those fabled ruins that once may have been the outposts of Sheba's empire.

"I think that you may have many interesting experiences," said His Highness. "I envy you and if it be the will of Allah that I am still alive when you return, then you must come and tell me about it. As for the real leviathans of the sea, I hope that you have sufficiently strong tackle." He went on to recount a most interesting story about a huge shark that had followed his yacht off the coast of Pemba Island. He had wished to shoot the brute but his captain had literally begged him to let well alone lest the monster, if wounded, should attack the little vessel. "My captain was probably unduly nervous of the results," he added. "But I must say that the sheer size of the shark seemed in some measure to justify his apprehensions."

On the conclusion of the Audience I accepted the good wishes of this kindly and devout man, the Sovereign of a happy land, as a good augury for the work and risks that lay ahead. The longer I live the more forcibly do I realize that the only men who are worth a button are those who live by the old rules of simple courtesy and kindliness, a code of human relationship that plays a less conspicuous part in the modern breed of men than in probably any generation of history; I have met these characteristics in elderly princes and in ancient beggars but in precious few of the younger generation, irrespective of class, and it augurs ill for the vintage of the future.

We came to know the little town fairly well and I must confess that, lacking that concentration of local colour which one finds so satisfying in Tangier, Zanzibar left an impression of only two physical characteristics — the beauty of the carved doors and a dearth of historic interest save for some of the Islamic tombs in the numerous graveyards.

The Arab population glided through their domestic and business lives with that combination of dignity and sense of worth which rightly places a higher value upon manners than on mere banking accounts. The Indians were as efficient, intense and specious as ever; and despite the perennial wet — wet sweat in sunlight, wet soak in the rain, a mental and physical dampness which saps the very life roots — the private European residents did their best to treat the stranger at the gate with that warmth of helpfulness and courtesy which once upon a time was actually to be found among representatives of British officialdom overseas. Though one comes across a little too much of *l'ingénue* in Zanzibar, expressed in a rather childish petulance which springs psychologically from the imprint of Government House doormat on the knees of certain officials, there is one proposed local measure which should be stopped at once by direct intervention on the part of the Colonial Office.

In defiance of an unwritten law, respected the world over by fishermen and humanitarians alike, the local Fisheries Department are equipping their new boat, which incidentally cost the wretched taxpayer some £ 5,000, with a shoulder harpoon gun for the purpose of slaughtering the porpoise for use as shark bait. A man who once committed a similar iniquity in Florida, hard-boiled though that coastline may be, was placed "in coventry" for a calendar year by every local sportsman and fisherman. And rightly so. To kill these friendly helpless mammals for shark bait is on a par with killing tame dogs in the street for lion bait. This monstrous proposal of the Fisheries Department has the approval of the Zanzibar government.

One evening Anna received a very special and gracious favour in the shape of an invitation to the marriage ceremony of the sixteen-year old daughter of an ancient Arab family of Muscat extraction who had settled generations before in the Sultanate of Zanzibar. No men were allowed to be present. Shortly after dark she found herself at the carved and spiked

entrance of a gaunt old Arab house where she was welcomed
by the bride's mother clad in a high-necked robe of magnificently embroidered silk beneath which peeped a pair of volu-
minous pantaloons. The outer room, a kind of salon with a
beamed ceiling, was filled with a mob of Arab and African
women clothed in a variety of strange colourful garments and
jewelled with barbaric necklets and bracelets blazing with the
glories of ancient craftsmanship. Everybody was chattering
and waving incense burners or dabbing perfumed oils on the
face and hands of each new arrival, and Anna was scented like
a lily within a minute of entering the room. The atmosphere
was almost intoxicating in its warmth and fragrance, for every
window was tightly closed against the threat of evil spirits, and
as she stood amid the blue haze of incense and the gleam of
strange gems and heavy rustling silks it seemed that some
magic carpet had wafted her back through the centuries into
the seraglio of the Thousand And One Nights.

She was still gazing absorbed in this display when the
mother seized her by the hand.

"Come to the Bride," she whispered, and led her to a door
opening into a smaller inner apartment.

This sanctum sanctorum was unfurnished save for a divan
and eight low stools on top of which were perched as many
small children clad in silken tunics and swinging little golden
incense burners. These details she saw in a glance before her
whole attention became riveted on the figure sitting alone upon
the divan. It was that of a young girl so rigidly motionless that
she might have been a corpse wrapped in cream satin and
weighed down with jewels. Her eyes were downcast, her hands
lay on her knees at exactly the same angles and her bare feet
rested precisely side by side on a velvet footstool. Her small
oval face was painted across the brow and chin with a design in

some brown coloured pigment, while her hands were literally covered with an elaborate scrollwork of scarlet and brown ending in gilded fingernails. A similar design and gilding decorated her bare feet.

It seemed as though a puppet of painted enamel rather than a creature of flesh and blood had been placed on the divan, a puppet that could neither speak nor move nor even flicker the long dark lashes that lay upon her powdered cheeks, and, as she contemplated that rigid little figure, Anna realized that here was one of those rare situations which are equally out of focus to the usually opposing factions of reality or romance. This bride-to-be of sixteen was to be married to a bridegroom of over sixty, and they had never even seen each other!

The thought had only passed through her head when the curtains over the doorway were pulled aside and the bridegroom himself entered the room. He was a powerful grey-bearded Arab resplendent in a turban and heavy scarlet silks encircled by a belt supporting a great curving dagger in a scabbard of chased silverwork. He took not the slightest notice of anybody but sitting down exactly opposite the bride who had not even raised her eyes — could any Western woman have endured this — for a quick peep at her future Lord and Master, he proceeded to contemplate her with the grave serenity of an entomologist surveying a satisfactory beetle. At length, he rose to his feet and as he held out his hand towards her she moved for the first time and placing her little fingers lightly on his, exactly in the style of the sixteenth century in Europe, they swept through the doorway into the main salon and so down an avenue of smiling women to another curtained arch through which they vanished but not before the quick opening and closing of the hangings had afforded a glimpse of an alcove empty save for a large bed.

The women laughed, chattered and jangled their bracelets and poured coffee from swan-necked jugs of exquisite Muscat brasswork inlaid with glowing copper. Anna was served with coffee and sweetmeats by old women, former slaves of the family, whose features were almost obscured by jewelled and richly chased nose ornaments of such size that they dangled over their mouths and chins. These old women took as much pride in the fact that originally they had been slaves of the house as the feudal retainer might display in speaking of the knightly family whose banner had led his forbears to battle.

As she made her way back through the narrow streets, fissures of deep blue shadow beneath overhanging balconies separated the one from the other by strips of star-filled sky, Anna wondered whether the ageless unchanging mosaic of the East might not be destined as the one element which had the depth of existence necessary to survive the Thing whose shade was already creeping inch by inch across the soul of the West.

CHAPTER 5

GATEWAY TO ADVENTURE

Our study of charts and maps had focussed the various problems of our adventure on to one point. If we were to accomplish anything, then we must have a boat of our own. Locally it was impossible to charter a vessel suitable for our specific purposes and so we had come face to face with the fact that either we were beaten at the very threshold of the Promised Land or we must dip deep into the old pouch. To cut a long story short, we discovered a boat lying in the harbour of Tanga on the coast of Tanganyika. I flew to the mainland and, at first glance, realized that here was the very ship for the job. She was a tough seaworthy little craft, 35 feet long and of 25 tons' weight and, like a gift from the Gods, equipped with a harpoon platform jutting from the bows. This was no time for hesitation and I bought her on the spot. Before leaving Tanga that evening on my return flight to Zanzibar I re-registered the little ship under the name of the *Gloria Scott*, a name which may ring a note of reminiscence among the students of Mr. Sherlock Holmes.

I shall long remember that return flight to Zanzibar. The sky and the glassy sea were merged into one great convex of fading iridescent light, sea shone on sky and sky on sea, so that we seemed to fly through the interior of a huge mother-of-pearl shell. Far below, like a sudden flaw in the opalescence, a circle of darkness showed where a Manta ray, after hovering batlike before the glory of the setting sun, had crashed back into the sea.

A few minutes later the pilot pointed to a tiny speck of coral islet that came floating out of the dimness.

"I've always felt that one should arrange a parachute descent there," he observed moodily. "Accompanied of course by the right woman."

I assented heartily. But a more hellish place with the wrong woman I could not have imagined.

The acquisition of the *Gloria Scott* obviously demanded a celebration and therefore as the only means for jollity offered by Zanzibar, that night we attended the cinema. A really low effort on the part of Hollywood was forgotten if not forgiven in view of the miraculous audience that graced the stalls and circle. Apart from two other white people, the patrons consisted of African negroes, in every conceivable form of clothing, duck-clad Indians, bearded Arabs including one sinister-looking gentleman in a djellabeh and a bedouin-style burnous cocked rakishly over one eye, and a whole phalanx of Arab women veiled from head to foot in impenetrable black and exactly resembling the masked horror of the Inquisition judges. Everybody talked incessantly, pausing only to break into wild applause whenever the Hollywood heroes shot each other. Even with such trifling things, in Africa one can never escape from the eternal element of contrast, so simply typified by the hot and roaring audience within and the cold stillness of the palm trees and the moon-washed road without.

The flurry of work following the arrival of the *Gloria Scott* in Zanzibar harbour became positively demoniacal. There was not a shelf nor a cupboard in the whole ship, the lavatory was a bucket and the cooking arrangements nil. So we set to work and out of emptiness and chaos and carpenter's dust, we made a habitable ship. The birth of the *Gloria Scott* was not, and is not, the birth of a luxury yacht. She became the very opposite,

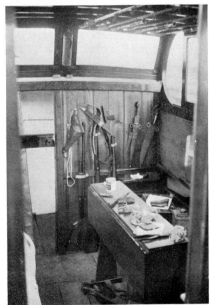

GLORIA SCOTT, CABIN AND FISHING CHAIR

GHILANI

JUM-JUM

a tough traditional type of adventure ship of the kind to delight the heart of every boy. The midship's cabin — oh, monstrous exaggeration—we turned into a galley which, though suitable in size for the munchkins of the Wizard of Oz, nevertheless met our needs. The walls of the main cabin gleamed with rows of rifles, revolvers, cartridge belts and great hunting knives for cutting the vertebrae and jaws from shark; the whole ceiling was raftered with big-game rods, while the underpart of the fixed settees were filled to bursting with nylon lines, shark ropes, ammunition, hundredweights of hooks and steel wire traces. What we fondly imagined to be a sufficiency of tinned goods and provisions were packed into the bilges. For sleeping quarters we relied on the top of the deck-house with canvas covers in the event of rain. Finally, amid the martial array of the main cabin, we fixed a couple of book shelves and from that moment were two lone adventurers no longer but a goodly company. Scott, Weyman, Conan Doyle, Machen, Charles Reade, Dickson Carr's Life of my father, all dog-eared old friends that would be with us to the end for better or for worse. How can we ever repay these men, the mighty Dead, whose creative output is the heritage whereby our smaller minds are enabled to peep over their mental shoulders to catch a glimpse of the Great Places through which their imaginations swept in ermine and in purple. May God bless and cherish them.

And now all was loaded, the plimsoll line below the water and the scent of adventure in our nostrils. An adventure it was going to be for, apart from big fish and deserted islands, our joint seamanship was probably sufficient to steer a punt across a very private lake. True, we had a seventy year old Arab Nahoda or captain and two African boys as engineer and cook, but as the Nahoda spoke not a word of English nor we of

4

Arabic except "Kismet" and "Allah akbad", expressions which seemed ill-chosen under the circumstances, our orders must consist of grins, grimaces and hurried drawings on scraps of paper. The whole affair was an affront to the dictates of common sense and therefore under the circumstances very right and proper.

We were moored during this busy period not in the polite waters where the visiting liners and various Government craft swing at their anchors but in the dhow harbour, down among the sea gypsies, where day means the warm perfume of drying cloves and night the crooning of arab voices and the red gleam of fires smouldering on the cooking slabs in the gaunt old vessels. Our first night aboard was a thing of blue magic. Lying together on the cabin top, which was our bed for the night, Anna and I looked up at a jewelled canopy patched with tiny puffs of cloud that shone in the moonlight like fragments of alabaster. Stark and straight as a silver lance, the mast rose above us, its bole encircled by a bristle of harpoon heads mounted on 12 foot Mango poles. The dark high-sterned shapes of the dhows surrounding our little ship on every side were carvings of jet on a sea of liquid silver glass. Somewhere a drum thudded softly; the world slept, and God was glorious in His heavens.

The few days and nights that remained to us in Zanzibar were simply packed with frights for amateurs like ourselves. We were of course living on board our tiny boat, that is to say Anna and I and Simmonds and an Arab odd-job boy, while our native crew slept on shore. Late one night or rather at two a.m. in the morning I finished some writing and came up for a breath of air. Everything was wrapped in sleep. In landlubberly style I leant over the rails wondering idly why the position of the breakwater lights had changed. And where were the dhows?

My yell roused the ship. We had dragged both anchors and were drifting stern first out to sea. I fear that our joint efforts to bring the ship back to her moorings would have appalled any self-respecting seaman, but to novices it was all very nerve-wracking in the middle of the night. Our guardian angels must have clocked in for a little overtime for, despite our bungling efforts to control swaying anchor-ropes and steer the ship, we succeeded eventually in returning to our anchorage without piling into another vessel or the breakwater. Silence, huge relief and the sleep of the just.

The very next evening an engineering acquaintance paid us a visit and, very much against my better sense, I listened to an insidious suggestion that now was the time, at twilight, mark you, to put to sea for a test. Up anchor and away we throbbed minus captain and crew. Two miles out in a rising sea and... bang! The main driving chain to the flywheel had broken. The comforting noise of the engine died away and an awful silence ensued broken only by the dash of the waves against our hull. The lights of Zanzibar twinkled in the distance. There was only one thing to do. Accompanied by our engineering visitor, I climbed into the dinghy, fixed a rope to the bows of the *Gloria Scott,* started the outboard motor and proceeded to tow her in. Rising and falling in the trough of the waves, the little dinghy was thrown about like a plummet at the end of a string. At one moment my companion's head would be in my stomach, at the next I would be up at the bows with the speed of a battering ram. A smell of singed flesh arose from the exhaust pipe of the outboard and swish! swish! swish! would come the tow-rope across the boat. By yelling "Port" or "Starboard", as the case might be, we managed to duck beneath the thwarts whenever the taut rope swept over the dinghy and though on three occasions we shipped so much water that we had to abandon the line in order to bail, at the end of three hours we had reached the safety of our anchorage and crept to bed, burnt, shaken and, personally speaking, aware of my existence merely as one large bruise.

However, within two days, such trifles were forgotten. All had been completed; fuel and water tanks filled to capacity; the bearded Arab Nahoda had taken his place behind the tiny wheel and the dark face of Mravile, our African engineer, smiled up at me from the engine-room hatch.

At 10.30 p.m. the Nahoda gave the signal and we hauled on the anchor ropes. The engine sprang to life and with the lights of Zanzibar slowly receding from sight and a trail of phosphorescence bubbling from our stern, we headed into the darkness of the open sea.

CHAPTER 6

THE LAMPS OF DEATH

It was a dreadful night. Three times the engine stopped owing to dirt from the fuel tank and the little ship wallowed helplessly in the swell of the sea. Mravile worked like a hero in an engine room swamped with the kerosene that was pouring from the tank, the top of which could not be kept in place owing to the violent movements of the ship until we wedged it in position by piling it with my heaviest steel fishing boxes.

The table was over, the galley floor rolling with tinned food, and the Bulldog, sensible creature, ensconced in a hurriedly found funk-hole under the cabin settee. Seldom have a group of people more fervently welcomed the first glimmer of dawn. It applies especially at sea that a situation which is positively appalling in the darkness becomes merely inconvenient in the rational light of day, and so it was in this case.

Our engine troubles were over by dawn and rolling and tossing for another six hours, we reached the calmer waters beyond Ras Kimbiji, and the glory of boiling hot tea crept over our souls. The sun was high and the sea blue and on our starboard side we had the companionship of the green coast of Africa. Ahead lay the beginnings of the Mafia channel.

We talked exultantly as we mounted rods and lines, and drank gallons of tea and coffee with promiscuous recklessness and gave Jum-Jum a meal that was three times too large for him. And through it all with never a break or a rest, motionless as a figure-head beautifully carved and chiselled in ancient wood, the patriarchal form of the Nahoda sat behind his tiny wheel.

Beyond the horizon the palms of far-off coral islets stood up with a curious rigidity just like clusters of telephone poles, but as we approached more nearly the low-lying beaches of sand became visible, each encircled by the white mutter of its own particular diadem of reefs.

These deserted islands were things of marvellous grace and beauty, but a beauty fraught with that strange elusive forlornness that belongs to Tinker Bell and the Never-Never Land.

We had mounted our very heavy dinghy across the stern and lashed it to the railings, which meant in effect that the big-game swivel chair was temporarily out of commission and the top of the dinghy became our perch for trolling. The wind was dying down but a fresh sea still running, so that one was staring up at a vividly blue sky one moment and down at a vividly blue sea the next — sky... sea... sky... sea — like the rocking of some monstrous cradle.

Crash! There was a vicious tearing strike on my line and I reeled in. The trolling lure, in this case a wooden plug resembling a squid, was untouched but the six-inch trolling lead showed the marks of savage teeth, very wide in the gap. I felt no doubt that it had been a Barracouda, one of the hated sea-wolves which wrought such appalling injuries during the war upon the victims of ships torpedoed in warm waters. These pike-like fish, averaging only three or four feet in length, are generally more dreaded than even the shark, for their mode of living is to attack every moving object with a slashing rip that tears the flesh from the bone and, as the Naval Authorities discovered in the bloody waters around the sinking refugee ships off the Gold Coast, the sea-wolf has a nice selectivity for the rounded parts of the body, especially the buttocks and breasts of women.

For some time we trolled without result, though flurries and sudden lines of splashes like a spray of machine-gun bullets tearing across the surface proved that there were plenty of game about.

I made my way for'ard to the harpoon platform rising and falling and heaving over the waves and had settled down to a pipe when my eye was caught by a tiny flash of colour some distance ahead. I watched carefully and sure enough it came again, a touch of vivid red in the foam of a breaking wave. I yelled to Anna, and there was just sufficient room for the two of us on the narrow steel-girt plank.

"Heaven knows what it is," I said. "There's no fish nor seaweed of that colour. Keep your eyes skinned and we may get another look at it."

Immediately in front of the bows a wave broke in a cascade of foam, leaving behind it an expanse of clear, brilliant blue.

"There... There!" cried Anna, pointing excitedly downwards but ahead. "Whatever is it?"

A few inches below the surface a most extraordinary object was floating towards us. Imagine to yourself a gigantic stocking more than six feet in length and of a red so blazing as to be almost luminous. Halfway down the smooth flat shape a horizontal white band divided the thing into two equal halves. It drifted slowly past, glowing brilliantly against the peacock blue water as though some gigantic witch of the sea had discarded one of her scarlet hose. I am still puzzled to classify this weird creature. Certainly it was neither fish nor jellyfish but bore a vague resemblance to a deep sea form of life known as the Venus Girdle. Most likely it was a variation of the latter.

"Think of having that folded up among your nylons," I observed to Anna.

She looked at me gravely: "Don't joke. I believe that we've seen something rare and wonderful."

"You're right," I agreed. "It was like the Venus Girdle except that it was neither white nor transparent. I can't place it."

Hour after hour we rolled along and the sun had begun to dip in the heavens when, as ill-luck would have it, at the moment when I was in process of climbing back on to the dinghy, there was a sudden burst of foam thirty yards behind the ship and, whang! my reel screamed, the rod bent like a whip and before I could even grasp the butt to make a sure strike, a magnificent Cavalli Jack rose in a tremendous leap. For an instant it hung in the air shaking its head from side to side, its silver body and yellow tail blazing in the sunlight, and then the lure flew from its jaws and a fountain of foam marked the disappearance of the victor.

Before we dropped anchor in the early evening under the lee of the tiny island of Kwale, I had lost two sets of tackle to really big fish that bit through the wire traces as if they were cotton. Though all the honours lay with the fish, it had been a thoroughly exhilarating day.

As soon as we were moored within the reef at Kwale a fisherman came out in his dug-out canoe and, in this, we went ashore to look the place over. It turned out to be a low island heavily wooded with palms, mangroves and fat-bodied Baobab trees looking rather like huge grey squids standing on their tails. At the edge of the lagoon was the traditional-type of palm-thatched village, a native Customs post and two rotting dhows. A dull safe place. At sundown, however, there was a strange sight to be seen.

In the far distance across the water the hill-tops of Tanganyika rose in a hard black outline against a sky of translucent orange fire shading down through airy terraces of flame and scarlet into a wonderful monotone of duck-egg green that seemed to soothe the world into one great placidity. By degrees this evening sky became peopled by flock after flock of large birds, all winging their way in complete silence from the woods of Kwale towards the distant mainland, and suddenly we realized that these were owls, literally thousands upon thousands of owls, death-bent towards the rustling forests of Tanganyika. For more than an hour they streamed overhead until the darkness hid their passage.

The night was very hot and breathless. Red lightning played and flickered incessantly along the whole circumference of the horizon and the stillness, huge and brooding, and broken only by that flicker of eerie light, touched primitive roots deep within one's being. In despite of reason, one quailed yet again before the tremendous dramatic sense that is always present in Nature, that eternal play between stillness and movement, colour against monotone and reality against reflection, which, simple in its constituents, is infinitely more awe-inspiring than the most dramatic and complicated situation that human genius is capable of devising.

Dawn rose on a calm sea and we headed down the Mafia channel, the little ship rolling along comfortably at a steady five knots. We trolled the whole time but, apart from one Kingfish hooked by Anna, well fought and finally lost after a magnificent display of leaping, we had no sport. By now, fresh food in the way of fish was badly needed and we were subsisting on tinned cheese, biscuits and cocoanuts while our water was warm and a cloudy red in colour. So weak tea became the order of the day. We were well into the Mafia and the coast of Africa had disappeared from sight. Islet after islet drifted by, all green feathers and virgin white sand and cascades of foam where the fangs of reefs broke the smooth blue run of the sea. Every hour was a freedom and an idyll.

In the afternoon after passing a lonely atoll composed entirely of sand without so much as a single palm we came upon a cluster of dhows anchored for fishing and as we swept past amid a welter of strange outlandish cries in Arabic and Swahili, the Nahoda suggested that, if we would spend the night at an island a few miles further on, we might join up with the dhows next day for a change of luck. Realizing that probably these fellows would know the local waters, I was much in favour of this suggestion and so we headed in the first flush of sunset for the little island and incidentally for one of the strangest experiences of my life.

Darkness had already fallen by the time that we had nosed our way gingerly through the reef-strewn waters and dropped anchor in the lagoon. At a few hundred yards distance the low black crescent shape stretched away for a half-mile on either side and throughout the whole line of the island the darkness was unbroken save for one feeble lamp glimmering in the hut of some lonely native fisherman. Sea and air were very calm and still and I could hear the low voices of my crew as they sat in the bows eating their evening meal of pineapples. We were attacking some bully-beef and biscuits in the cabin by the light of a hurricane lantern when Simmonds came down the hatchway with a queer look on his face.

"I have just seen Something, about twelve feet long, swim past the ship," he said, "It was lit up with green fire."

We bounded on deck. Save for the brilliant stars and that one feeble glimmer on the shore the darkness was infinite. On peering over the side, however, I noticed a kind of luminous twinkle, like fragments of star dust, gleaming and vanishing and gleaming again in the blackness of the water. This was mere phosphorescence and I was proceeding to remark on that fact to Simmonds in emphatic terms, when seizing my arm he pointed into the darkness.

"A lot of nonsense, eh? Well explain that," he cried exultantly — "There, over there! My God, what is it?"

At some distance away on the starboard beam, there had
appeared a mass of glowing luminosity moving slowly towards
the ship.

"*What is it?*" he repeated.

"I'm damned if I know. Never saw anything like it before."

Silently, we stood and watched. It was apparent that this
great patch of light, burning with a weird electric blue colour,
was well below the surface of the sea and, as it moved nearer,
the whole ship beneath the waterline commenced to glow with
the radiance of its approach. It was passing directly under the
keel when, seizing a lead sinker from the deck, I hurled it into
the depth. In an instant the whole mass disintegrated into
tongues of blue flame streaking away like meteors through the
blackness of the water.

"Great Scott!" ejaculated Simmonds. "It's a school of big
fish."

"Right. But it is the light that puzzles me. In the normal way
phosphorescence... My heavens, man, look at that!"

"And over there!" cried Anna — "there too. Oh, what a
marvellous sight!"

From all directions slow-moving masses of submarine light
had begun to drift about the lagoon, glimmering palely at a
distance of some hundred yards and gradually warming into
wonderful shades of blue and green as they moved nearer to the
ship. We hung spellbound over the railings. By watching very
closely it was possible to discern that some of these mobile
patches of light were caused by great sharks while others were
whole schools of middle-sized fish. I cast out and my line
was a thread of green fire in the blackness of the sea. As I
reeled in and cast a second time, the run of the moist line

actually lit up the whole length of my rod with ghostly radiance. A hundred yards away two luminous shapes drifted past slowly and stealthily through the darkness.

"Those are two really big Barracouda," I said. "Now watch!"

I cast out again and as my spinner hit the surface there came a swirl of fire as the sea-wolves hurled themselves around and sped for the kill. I wound in steadily but, alas, the distance was too great and the jaws of the nearest pursuer, luridly flickering with light, were three feet distant when the spinner bumped against the side of the ship. By the time that I cast out again, the things had plunged and vanished under the *Gloria Scott*.

"If you fell overboard in this lagoon, you'd be lucky if you lasted twenty seconds," Anna whispered, "It's the most eerie, fascinating horror that I've ever seen."

"Yes. They are Coleridge's witchlights come to life."

We fell silent, each affected in his own way by the weird atmosphere of menace that seemed to hem us in.

Our tiny ship had become quite suddenly an island of life floating on an immensity of darkness and death. Jum-Jum, snuffling and blowing as he peered through the rails with his ears cocked, was dragged away unceremoniously and locked below in the cabin.

Sheets of fire, swift and shimmering, rushed under our keel and were varied from time to time by the single fluorescent outline of some killer of the Deep ravening through the haunted waters in pursuit of its prey or nosing and circling amid the bubbles of its own wake that streaked the surface like a filigree of moonstones.

More than once the brooding hush enwrapping the night was broken by a loud booming as though some giant had smitten the sea with the flat of his hand, and we conjectured that these mysterious sounds were caused by Manta ray, great batlike creatures measuring up to 30 feet across, which have a habit of rising straight up into the air and after hovering for a few moments falling flat upon the surface of the sea.

"Well, I've never seen anything like this off the coast of Australia," Simmonds observed quietly. "We get a lot of phosphorescence in the Pacific, but these lights are all below the surface."

"What causes these conditions I cannot imagine, but it is certainly not a case of normal phosphorescence such as one might expect in tropic waters," I agreed. "Some years ago I experienced an astonishing phosphorescence one night off the coast of Spanish Guinea when, for three miles, we ploughed through a sea of solid green fire and I was able actually to read a newspaper on the top deck of a 6000 ton ship through the luminosity raised by the bow waves." It was a memory of unearthly beauty. But this black lagoon with its prowling patches of light moving and vanishing and reappearing beneath the glass-calm surface of the water belonged to a different category.

The hours passed, Simmonds had turned in long since, and at length Anna retired to rest. The thought of sleep was impossible, so I climbed on to the cabin roof and smoking pipe after pipe sat enthralled before the pageantry of that strange lagoon and, sure enough, in the hour before dawn, there came the climax.

The moving masses had become markedly fewer and I was on the point of descending from my eyrie when suddenly there appeared far away beyond the bows of the ship a distant patch of submarine luminescence of immense size. Nearer it came, and nearer, and now I could count no less than three great disturbances of greenish light proceeding in line formation one behind the other.

Straight past the ship they swept, their diamond-shaped-forms lit up in a livid radiance, their great flukes thirty feet or more from tip to tip and so on into the darkness, streaming with heatless fire like ghost coaches gliding. Thus passed the Mantas.

I retired for an hour's rest under a piece of canvas, but sleep was out of the question for my mind was racing with the extraordinary spectacle which I had had the luck to witness. It was worth a journey across the world.

CHAPTER 7

WORLD RECORD

We were up anchor at dawn and away to join the dhows for a day that was a complete anti-climax from every point of view. In vain we fished for hours under a pitiless sun. The sea itself seemed to sizzle in the heat and the panting of poor Jum-Jum had to be relieved by buckets of salt water regularly poured over him. The reward of our labours consisted merely of one Remora or Sucker fish the proportions of which gave one to ponder on the probable size of the sharks which could carry a parasite nearly three feet in length. The Remora is a curious creature with a slim, tor-pedo-shaped body and along the top of its head a thing like a rubber tennis shoe sole, size twelve. This is the sucker by which it clings to the bellies of shark and rays, and thus obtains free board and transport throughout the marine highways — a kind of Whitehall official in disguise.

Towards evening the weather chilled perceptibly and the wind began to rise. The dhows had scattered in the gloom and owing to our own stupidity in delaying too long on the fishing ground we were able to get only a part of the way back to the island before the Nahoda decided that he dare not allow the ship to travel further owing to the menace of the reefs in the darkness. So, having no alternative than to drop anchor in the open sea, we spent a miserable night rolling and pitching and in a state of nervous tension, Jum-Jum alone snoring his way peacefully through the nocturnal watches. At daylight hot tea and bully beef whipped up our spirits and with the wind falling away into a still calm we were off once more, quietly chugging along through a dream world of coral islands and serene blue distances. Suddenly the waters ahead and on either side were lashed by bursts of spray as school after school of Kingfish commenced to feed on leaping swarms of fry. The whole surface of the sea literally boiled with fish. But could we catch any? Again and again we trolled right through the centre of the schools and could actually see the fine 25 lb. fish darting about on either side of our little vessel. And nary a strike! It was infuriating to a degree of madness. The old Nahoda did his best by zig-zagging the *Gloria Scott* all over the ocean in wild pursuit of the various schools, but all in vain and one almost expected to hear silvery laughter rising from the sea. Then I had a strike and a Kingfish broke water fighting gamely. He was firmly hooked and there was no excuse for the fact that I lost him. An instant of slack on the star-drag during his initial run and he was gone like a flash. A piece of rank bad fishing on my part, and it remained now for a woman to regain the honour of the ship. Smash! Anna's rod bent like a reed and the reel screamed wildly as the line went ripping off behind the run of a really fast fish. A hundred yards, two hundred yards, then in a burst of spray a long silver shape leapt into the air.

"Barracouda!" I cried. "Get him, for heaven's sake!"

Anna made no mistakes. Very coolly she fought the brute for some twenty minutes before she brought it within reach of the gaff. It was wrenched on board, snapping like a wolf and sent to the shades of its ancestors with a hearty blow from a New Guinea war club. It was a really vicious looking specimen and topped the scales at 35 lbs. The importance of this fish lay in the fact that now we had not only some fresh food but more urgent still good trolling bait. I have found that there is no lure

ANNA

A.C.D. ON HARPOON PLATFORM

MRINI, 5 P.M., OVER KILWA KISIWANI

AUTHOR'S SKETCH OF THE MANTA RAYS AT NIGHT

in the world to beat the white flesh from the stomach of a Barracouda.

One of the crew had omitted to screw tight the tap of the water supply tank and, as a result, the larger part of our drinking water had vanished during the night. This damnable piece of carelessness threatened to place the whole ship's company in danger, situated as we were with an uncertain engine and no sails in an area of mostly waterless islands. I put the offender on parched rations for two days, so that he might sample a taste of what might yet come in a far more serious form. Continuous small troubles in the engine room had reduced our speed considerably and for two days we rationed ourselves strictly in the consumption of our precious water.

Then shortly after dawn, we sighted a small island so luxuriantly covered with vegetation that it seemed certain that there must be springs or some other form of natural irrigation. Ghilani, however, who claimed that he knew the island by repute, eyed its green waving beauty with the utmost distaste and uttered the one word 'Chattu' (Python).

Arming myself with a .45 Webley revolver and a machete for cutting the bush, I went ashore in the dinghy and scrambling up a ledge of rock plunged into the emerald gloom of the jungle. For jungle it was, certainly not bush. High trees interlacing overhead almost shut out the sunlight, while festoons of lianas and air plants drooping from the branches with a stealthy febrile grace conveyed the impression of living entities poised momentarily in their contortions. I followed a narrow stone watercourse, now quite dry, and very fortunate I was in finding this, for it would have been out of the question to cut a path with my machete through the matted wall that hemmed me in on either side.

The undergrowth was prolific, bristling with spiky branches

5

and wait-a-bit thorns and adorned with sudden vivid splashes of colour where a red-leaved shrub smouldering in the walls of green, dropped its foliage like cascades of tiny bloody shields above a curious fat-leaved plant resembling a gigantic Lily of the Valley. Birds were plentiful, evincing not the slightest fear of my presence, while in the stretches of eternal twilight where the watercourse ran under tunnels of overhanging boughs, flocks of bats wheeled and flitted boldly about my head. It was obvious that the murder instincts of man were as yet unknown to the inhabitants of this tiny fragment in the sea.

Several times I was aware of cautious rustling movements in the undergrowth accompanied by a sudden nodding of foliage disturbed by the passage of something or other. Drawing my revolver I kept my eyes on the branches overhead, for the python has a habit of hanging by its tail like a piece of dead wood and dropping upon its victim as he passes below. At length, I broke through to a sandy cove at the other side of the island and it was here that I came upon silent evidence which caused me to eye the wall of jungle behind me with heightened alertness.

The sand was literally covered with the marks of snakes! Over a stretch of less than a hundred yards I counted no less than eighteen separate snake tracks, winding and twisting amid the remains of smashed sea-shells and the pulp of crustacea, and ranging in size from the breadth of a whip lash to that of a motor tyre. It was now amply evident that the island was swarming with snakes of several different varieties. But how on earth did they live? Birds, rodents and bush babies were scarcely likely to be in sufficient quantity to offer a supply of food adequate to the needs of a host of reptiles. I can only think that here we have another of Nature's wonderful readjustments to meet local conditions, and that the shells on the shore, ever replaced by a fresh supply driven from the outer reef, were in the habit of being crushed by the snakes and then swallowed for their rich meaty contents. I can see no other explanation.

My search for water was unsuccessful, though there must have been springs hidden away somewhere in the jungle. The best I could find was a mere pool of amber-coloured liquid stinking of death in a bowl-shaped rock. Having discovered another dried runnel leading in the right direction, I headed back for the ship. The dim luxuriant monotony seemed to press down on me with a stifling sense of stagnation and, pouring with sweat, I had to remind myself constantly of the marks on the sand to preserve some degree of mental clarity. At one point only was the oppressive drowsiness engendered by the combination of heat and moisture banished before a vision of such transcendent loveliness that one could only gape and tremble. From a single tree jutting forth into the sunlight from the shadow-world below there hung a golden curtain of orchids. Perfumeless, they were flowers without souls and yet in that place of shades and leaves and lavish desolation, they smote upon the senses like the blaze of a chandelier in the labyrinth of some ruined catacomb.

When I regained the shore I headed along the edge of the island toward the spot where I had left the dinghy. At first glance the narrow expanse of coral sand blazing white in the sunlight seemed desolate and lifeless but as I trudged on I became aware that the whole surface of the beach was shimmering with the movement of tiny creatures. Legions of dark pebbles moved en masse, froze into immobility, and then moved again so slowly that I doubted the evidence of my own eyes until a closer examination identified my pebbles as a vast host of sea-snails. These curious little molluscs, each encased in its green, brown or particoloured shell, were engaged on hard forced marches of a few inches at a time to reach the shelter of the sea before the heat literally fried the life out of them. There seemed to be a movement of rather larger swifter things criss-crossing the shore beyond the sea-snail army but as I approached nearer these scurrying objects melted so quickly into the sand that they appeared to dematerialise. I stood very still and waited. There was not a movement nor a sound save for the soft breathing of the sea at the edge of the coral strand. Then, as though with a single impulse, the whole surface of the sand bristled with hundreds of weird tiny shapes that clawed and clambered from invisible holes. They were Fiddler crabs, once seen never to be forgotten. These specimens were black in colour streaked and patched with white, so that they resembled fragments of a zebra's hide. Though the left claw was normal, the right one was developed into a fearsome scythe-shaped weapon almost as large as the crab itself and of a lovely rose pink. The females could be easily distinguished by their generally more decorous behaviour and their lack of the great claw, but the males bullied, bustled and strutted, holding their huge ungainly nippers like shields across their fronts and making frequent slashes at each other or pausing to brandish their armament in the air as though to challenge the Deity Himself to mortal combat amid the ripples of sand and broken sea shells. Between bouts of ill-temper, they were the busiest people in the world, shovelling sand out of their tunnel homes and scavenging every minute scrap of food in the shape of odd fish scales and bits of polyp and debris. The males were love-conscious to a degree of downright vulgarity and fortunately for the peace of the beach they had never acquired the American wolfwhistle, for every time that a female crawled into sight every male in the vicinity would rise on his toes and brandish his great claw as high as he could reach. And then, in the midst of all this fascination of black and white and pink and eating and flirting, I made a tiny movement and in an instant the beach was as empty and lifeless as a slab of cement.

I had rounded the point when I saw Anna coming toward me.

"How did you get ashore?" I asked.

"Ali fetched me in the dinghy," she replied. "He returned for the shotgun to try to knock down some coconuts. Look at this exquisite shell which I found. Isn't it exactly like a Greek vase."

One glance was enough at the lovely delicate thing mottled all over with white and amber scrollwork and then I hit her hand so sharply that the shell rolled ten yards away.

"What...!"

"I am sorry, but there was not a moment to lose. You were holding it by the wrong end."

"But I don't understand," she cried, "I've collected scores of different shells and they're all perfectly harmless." She looked at me indignantly. "I want my Greek vase, so would you mind picking it up."

"Certainly, by the right end and wrapped in a bit of cloth. This is a Conus. Now, just watch and for God's sake remember!"

I poked a piece of stick into the narrow base of the vase and as I withdrew it a wickedly barbed greenish-coloured blade flickered out, stabbed the air and recoiled into the shell as though drawn by a spring.

"Good Heavens!" she cried. "It's got a horrible little dagger tucked away inside."

"Unfortunately it is something a damn sight worse than a dagger," I observed. "It is a hypodermic syringe loaded with a poison which is quite capable of killing a human being."

"But what are we to do? There are lots of these shells — you've never seen such glorious shapes and designs in your life apart from the real Greek vases — over there in the shallow waters. We must have some specimens."

"Well, we'll pick them up by the broad ends and throw them in my knapsack. Let's go and have a look."

The shallows were richly carpeted in a variety of green and red seaweeds and algae bejewelled with small discs of clear polished colours as though handfuls of guineas and turquoises had been scattered over the tresses of the sea. These dome-shaped discs, enamelled in deep glowing gold or blue fading into a pearly white, were Money Cowries, a type of shell used for centuries past as an international currency throughout Africa and Asia. They were, and in some places still are, the valid coinage of Nature's own special Mint. Here and there, amid the crevices of the coral, lay the graceful forms of the Conus shells as perfect in their symmetry as the ancient products of Athens and Mitylene and glowing in wonderful patinas of orange banded with white or laced with designs delicate as spiders' webs laid on surfaces of polished fawn-coloured glass. Across the more luxuriant expanses of algae moved specimens of the *Cassis Rufa,* shells as large as grapefruit and looking rather like elfin houses hewn out of rose-red marble. The finest cameos are made from a small portion of these shells, for which purpose they are exported to Italy from the Indian Ocean, but only the males can be used owing to the added thickness of their surface. There seems to be an unfortunate allegory tucked away somewhere.

Anna was lucky in securing a very fine sample of *Turbo Mamoratus,* a shell which usually inhabits rather deeper waters and in consequence carries more than its fair share of tube worms, parasite growths and other marine disfigurements. This particular specimen was a great green-mottled goblet lined with brilliant mother-of-pearl protected by a veritable front-door of some heavy stone-like substance which opens or slams shut at the will of the molusc living within. As we were examining this shell, I noticed that we had been joined by a young Barracouda about eight inches in length. I had heard much about the absolute fearlessness of these dangerous fish and so I put this baby to the test by striking at it with Anna's iron-pointed staff. I could have saved myself the trouble. Where any other fish, short of a man-eating shark, would have fled for its life this little devil stayed put, merely avoiding the blows and remaining all the while within a few inches of our legs. It had no fear, much curiosity and, I am quite sure, a vague atavistic prompting to associate those strange white stalks with something good to rend and chew.

Enriched with our sea-spoils, we splashed our way back to the shore where, after our cool wading, the temperature smote upon us in a scorching blast of heat waves through which the outline of the jungle danced and shimmered as though made of green jelly.

On reaching my original landing point, we found that Ali had managed to gather a few coconuts, the milk of which represented a valuable addition to our drinking supplies, and so the best that we could do was to push on for some other island which might contain a well.

A freshening wind towards mid-day broke the wave tops into spurts and hisses of foam which did nothing to improve the fishing conditions. I had just mounted big-game tackle, a very foolish procedure considering my wholly unsuitable position perched on the top of the lashed dinghy high above the ship's rail, when there came a tremendous strike, over went the rod tip and the line was torn out in a screaming blur. I strained back with all my strength, tightening the star drag brake but failed to make a whit of difference. Out whizzed the line for three hundred yards and crouched on the end of the ding- hy, it was touch and go whether I pulled in the fish or the fish pulled in me! Dexterously, Anna managed to slip the braces across my shoulders and round the arm-pits and thus I was able to bring the upper part of my body into the battle. The engine had been shut down to its slowest and for more than half an hour the fight lasted without a pause or a let up. The fish fought like a maniac, plunging deep, rising in a wild rush towards the surface and then tearing away in a great circle that ripped the line from the reel with a long high-drawn shriek. The speed was terrific. Vaguely I knew that I was deal- ing with sinew rather than weight, that here was a game fish par excellence, something that would fight as the thorough- bred horse will run, until the bursting of its noble heart. My muscles were on fire, while in sharp contrast my hands had be- come numb claws fighting, correcting, braking only through instinct. A vague terror shot through my brain that someone might touch the rod, try to assist — "Damn you, keep away! keep away!" I yelled in all the blind fury of one who is just clinging on by his finger nails. "I'll get the bastard!" In fact, there was nobody within ten feet of me.

Sometimes I gained a few yards only to slow up as a dead weight pulled at the other end of the line as though the fish had turned on its side to add breaking strain, then the braces bit into my shoulders like two hot wires as the fish wrenched off another hundred yards of nylon in a magnificent curving run that brought the water spurting from the taut line as it tore in a huge semi-circle across the wake of the ship.

For an instant in a smother of foam I caught a momentary

glimpse of my opponent and thought him a yellow-fin Tuna. A few minutes later, however, he broke surface again and this time I saw that unforgettable flash of emerald green, shimmering blue and gold, that to the fisherman spells two words — Dorado Dolphin, one of the gamest Gamefishes in the world. And this fighting fish must under no circumstances be confused with that homely old mammal, the porpoise. It is no relation.

At length, aching in every limb I brought him alongside and so on board. What a glorious thing he was, with his blunt golden head and tapering body shimmering all over with iridescent colours. I had caught far bigger fish of other types but never such a fighter. We would have removed the hook and put him back in the sea, the gallant fellow, were it not for the fact that we really needed the food.

But was this not an outsize in Dolphins? Certainly I had seen a few of similar length but none of that body depth. It couldn't be... surely, it was not possible... We weighed it carefully on the fishing scales; then we weighed it again. It was exactly 75½ lbs; 8 lbs heavier than the World Record Dolphin caught six years previously.

I may add that on our arrival at Kilwa Masoko, our scales were rechecked and found to be correct, whereupon I swore an affidavit with the testimony of five witnesses and entered my claim for the new World Record with the International Game Fish Association headquarters in New York. And a few weeks later came the splendid news that my fighting Dolphin of the Mafia Channel was indeed the official new World Record. May he flourish for ever in the Valhalla of sportsmen.

Shortly after the excitement had subsided Simmonds played and landed a very nice little Kingfish of 15 lbs which was the best eating of the day.

We were by this time becoming rather worried about our
night anchorage when the Nahoda, with a grunt of satisfaction, pointed to a smudge on the horizon, and a hasty examination of the charts showed that this must be the islet of Songo
Songo complete with a well. The sun was sinking rapidly and
as we neared the island the black silhouette of the palm trees
was boldly limned against a smouldering copper-red sky. We
dropped anchor on the edge of the reef, and rest and fresh water
seemed comfortably in sight when there came a bump, followed by a horrible crunching noise beneath the keel. Our anchor
had slipped and we were on the coral! I have seldom moved so
fast in my life. Man, woman — I almost added, and dog — we
pulled at the anchor chain with all our strength while Mravile
strove to restart the engine against a devil's tattoo of bangs and
thuds that brought our hearts into our mouths. For to a ship
coral is death. We managed to warp her forward a few feet in
the process of which two flukes of the forward anchor were
forced nearly straight, and then the engine sputtered and started and a few minutes later we were free. Suddenly a voice hailed us through the night and a dug-out canoe, replete with the
Headman of Songo Songo and his acolytes, swept alongside.
The Headman presented a fine, portly figure in a species of
white nightgown and, as we had not one word in common save
Pa Pa which is Swahili for shark, I led him down into the cabin
and there attempted to obtain local information by showing
him detailed drawings of various types of shark, marlin and
sawfish. It was a scene for Rembrandt. The yellow light of the
lantern lighting up in bold relief the grim features of the Chief
as he frowned over the sketches glinted in the background on
the impassive ebony figures of my two Africans while, like the
face of a bearded hawk outlined against a patch of stars, the
Nahoda's head peered down through the open hatch. I smoked

and watched them in the dim glow while they muttered and mumbled together over the names of great fish, and the information that we eventually received warranted a return to the neighbourhood of Songo Songo.

The next day would see us south of the Mafia Channel and on the last stage of our journey to Kilwa Masoko. The dawn rose sullenly and soon after our departure we ran into a concentrated downpour of rain, and the piling clouds on the horizon did nothing to improve matters. The sea was rising rapidly and soon the little boat was staggering through a series of waves that tossed her about like a cork. The ocean was out for mischief and it was all that we could do to keep on our feet. The table was over, carrying the floor boards with it, and the scene in the galley was beyond description, cans and kettles everywhere and my shaving brush, heavily loaded with soap, deep in the heart of a sack of onions. Jum-Jum was back in his old funk-hole and, had there been room, probably we should have all crept in with him. As it was, we just held on and cheered up each other with palpable lies about breaks in the clouds and lessening seas. Our world seemed to consist of a never ending welter of spray, crashes and groaning timbers. Metaphorically I took off my hat to that bold-hearted little ship. She fought magnificently every foot of the way and by the time that dusk was falling she had gained the mouth of the Kilwa estuary, and was heading up a lovely tranquil stretch of water bounded on one side by the waving palms and undergrowth of Southern Tanganyika and on the other by the thick green bush of the island of Kilwa Kisiwani. The first lap of our adventure had come to an end. But the real work still lay ahead.

CHAPTER 8

MIDNIGHT MAN-EATER

It was Christmas Eve. A ripple of lightning flickered unceasingly across a grey sky, hanging low and hot above the dull green jungle of Ras Mashindo, while a wind, bitter with the stench of rotting vegetation, churned the water into a dirty monotone and added its forlorn moaning to the loneliness of the place and the day. A long-necked Pepper bird gliding over the channel stood out with the starkness of a black crucifix against the heavens and might have symbolized the tragic genius of Poe, hovering in dreams over just such a spot when he wrote:

"And the red winds are withering in the sky."

Anna and I were now alone save for our native crew. Simmonds had returned to Australia, and we lay at Ras Mashindo, a lonely stretch of jungle-girt water notorious for sharks in the upper reaches of the Kilwa estuary.

In fact, the fishing was rotten, and apart from a young White Shark, which I landed on the rod, the only big specimen had wrenched himself free from the shark line in the early hours of the morning, and since then the silence had been absolute save for the growling of thunder and the rattle of petrol tins as one or other of us would search for a mugful of stinking tomato-coloured water to slake our thirst.

Christmas Eve! The thought kept recurring to me very much against my will and for the first time I was conscious of an almost overwhelming depression. My work, my objectives, my hopes were all equally futile and meaningless. None of this should be written and yet I wish this document to be a true record not only of our physical adventures but of the mental reactions that play so fundamental a part in all human experiences. Thanks to my parents, this period of the year was particularly rich in its memories, and the faces that passed now before my mental eyes against a background of roaring fires and holly and pink-shaded lamps were, with only two exceptions, the features of the so-called dead. It was they, and the music of their lives, that had given me those remembrances that now rose like beloved ghosts to obscure the flicker of the hurricane lamp on the table and the dull glint of the rifle barrels on the wall of the little cabin. What lasts in this world except one's memories and the yearning to find... Something; an unknown place, the way to another planet or the love of a human heart? I felt restless and depressed. Perhaps, at that time and in that place, it was a far-off reflection of the candle glow at the altars of a man's childhood.

But to proceed with our story. I could cover our experiences of the past fortnight in one miserable line. We had lain keel-rotting at Kilwa Masoko, unable to move owing to engine trouble. Day after day and the same jetty, the same native boy fishing from the end of it and the same monotonous green of the Mkoko trees at the water's edge; night after night working by lanterns amid the heat and the thudding of the drums from the shore and the everlasting flicker of lightning that reflected on the water the whole panorama of the heavens. Far off towards Ras Mashindo a solemn glow in the sky pulsed and reddened where the lightning had struck the bush. Food and sleep hardly counted in the face of the awful fact that our plans were held up and the bowels of our engine littering the deck. It was a time of strain for all of us. The Nahoda, a man of the deepest religious feelings, who throughout the expedition never failed at sundown in that sincere and beautiful expression of his Faith that bows the head and lifts the hands in adoration towards the West, became so wrought upon that he actually raised his venerable beard above the open engine-room hatchway in a fervent appeal to Allah Himself. Ali, a most likeable specimen of seaman cum cookboy, moved moodily about his duties while giving voice to most mournful songs. One night, while working in the engine-room, I paid rather more attention to the crooning that floated down from the deck above and suddenly realised that I was listening to Africanised versions of rebel Jacobite airs of the eighteenth century.

"Where did you learn these songs?" I asked, thrusting an oil-streaked face through the hatchway.

"I larn 'em from good man in Zanzibar, sah," replied Ali. "Very holy man, sah!"

"Do you realise, you rogue, that you are demanding the return of the Bonnie Stuart?"

A huge but uncomprehending grin split the darkness.

"He comes, sah," he cried consolingly, "he come!"

We were visited often by natives bearing news of great Pa Pa (shark), of Pa Pa Panga (sawfish) and of Mta (Manta ray) to add to our misery, so that we worked like snapping demons and finally succeeded in starting the engine. Out to sea we went only to find that we had a maximum speed of one knot per hour and could not even make headway against the waves. So back again, and more work and eventually the trouble was overcome, and we were mobile at long last, and straining upon the leash. And on that day the weather changed and the great winds came upon the sea turning the hitherto smiling mouth of the estuary into a savage white grin. During the time that the wind lasted there was only one thing to do, so we headed up the inland waters thickly girded with bush un-

touched by man, to test the sharky reputation of Ras Mashindo amid the red lightning and the loneliness of Christmas Eve.

Anna and I celebrated Christmas Day by making our way
in the outboard dinghy through the various channels stretching between the islands around Ras Mashindo. Protected by
thick jungle, the beautiful avenues of water lay as smooth as
sword blades; not even a fish broke the calm grey surfaces.
But they were far from silent, for every now and then there
came from beneath the shadows of the overhanging Mkoko
trees a series of rumbles and belches as though the water's edge
was lined with portly gentlemen recovering from the effects of
a Lord Mayor's banquet. Thus did the hippopotami make their
august presence known to us. Landing, we pushed some distance inland through a country of great trees intersected with
patches of green turf, that showed plentiful traces of game and
at one point we came upon the spoor of a leopard which must
have been of exceptional size, for the pud marks were nearly
as large as those of a lion. We were later than I intended on our
return and the short twilight was already falling as we neared
the place where the dinghy was beached. The roarings and
gruntings of the hippos in the water among the Mkoko trees
seemed disconcertingly close and, knowing their somewhat
unreliable tempers, I had unslung my rifle for safety's sake
when, at that instant, there came a sudden crashing through
the bush as though a tank was charging down upon us from the
landward side. Throwing all dignity to the winds, we ran like
greyhounds for the dinghy and, shoving off, leapt aboard as
the hippo rushed into the Mkoko trees a few yards away. It
was no joke at the time, for a hippo is a very nasty customer if
you get between him and the water. On Mafia Island some
months later I heard the story of a man who has a most pecu-
liar silhouette when standing up. The poor devil was chased by

a hippo tamus which eventually overhauled him and with one snap bit off his backside! It is really outrageous that tragedy is so often tinted with the ludicrous.

That night we held high wassail on the *Gloria Scott* by opening a tin of chicken for our Christmas dinner, garnished with spinach and washed down with flagons of piping tea, over which fare Anna made a gracious as well as a lovely hostess, I an excellent host, and Jum-Jum a grateful if importunate guest!

The lights of our tiny ship were a mote of human life in a vast primeval world of black sky and blacker jungle illumined periodically by flashes of lightning, like sudden glimpses of a savage picture daubed in burnished copper. Thus passed our Christmas.

Shortly after dawn a native in a seagoing dug-out canoe came up the channel in search of us with a story which made us reach for our harpoons. It seems that on the previous evening, when he had been wading in the shallows of Lindi-Sewa, a treacherous channel between the islands of Kilwa Kisiwani and Songa Manara, a huge shark had attempted to reach him. Fortunately the man had been only a few feet from the shore, hence his escape; but he was still dreadfully agitated, and when he added that this shark was known to patrol the channel and the inland waters beyond and that it had eaten the crew of a small dhow which had capsized, we felt that here was a sign and, should the winds permit, that very day would see us at the fabulous island of Songa Manara. I use the word fabulous advisedly.

The rumour of great ruins mouldering in the green twilight of the jungle, ruins seen by only few white men, excavated by none, not even properly examined; the remote possibility that this little coral island was once linked with that strange and beautiful woman whose love for King Solomon illumined their period of history and inspired the writings of the Ancients; surely here were siren lips to call a man.

That Sheba herself came to Songa Manara is unthinkable, but the shadow of her sceptre might still lie in the heart of the jungle.

Let us consider the known facts, which are few indeed among the mythological mist which has shrouded the still unknown coast of East Africa for the past 3,000 years. A thousand years before Christ, Kilwa and Songa Manara, like all the other coral islands off the coast of Africa, formed part of that portion of Sheba's Empire known as Tharish. With the flowering of her love for Solomon and her ensuing interest in his projects, Sheba the Woman used the power of Sheba the Queen to offer practical expression of that interest in her lover's work by despatching emissaries, complete with fleets, to the furthest corner of her realms to procure gold, ivory and precious stones for the adornment of the Great Temple of God. Today it is a generally accepted fact that the ruins of Zimbabwe in Africa are nothing less than the Ophir of the Scriptures — King Solomon's Mines — from which £ 75,000,000 of gold were taken. Ruined Kilwa (the Quiloa of the Ancients), mentioned by Milton in *Paradise Lost* as a part of the southern empire, was originally one of the coastal strong points, though the treasures were actually shipped from Salala in the Mafia Channel. Incidentally in one afternoon, working merely with a coral pick and two hunting knives Anna and I unearthed a human skull, early pottery and richly coloured beads amid the Kilwa ruins.

Although ancient documents clearly define the final development of Kilwa by the Shirazi-Persians a thousand years ago, the neighbouring island of Songa Manara is not even mentioned. This omission is particularly intriguing in view of the fact

6

that the ruins on Songa Manara are probably of greater anti-
quity and certainly of much greater pomp and glory than those
of Kilwa-Kisiwani, and represent no mere trading post but a
great palace with all the panoply and far-flung structural domain that the word implies.

Did its creation spring from the orders of the great Queen?
Who dwelt beneath its regal roof, and why? When did it
begin, and when did it end? And again why?

From the first I had determined to get there, to this island
with a name like the thrum of a harpstring, to this island with
a secret. And now, with the slackening of the wind, my opportunity had come.

"Allah! Allah! Allah!" chanted the crew in unison with the
hoisting of the anchor chain. Slowly the jungled mounds of
Ras Mashindo slid away and passing down the long stretch of
inland water we reached the open sea. On the way along the
coast we took a severe buffeting and in the Lindi Sewa channel
the following swell towered high above our stern. When I see
this kind of thing, I always realize how much I like the land. A
few hours later however we were safely round the point and
our anchor rattled down in relatively calm waters.

A hundred yards distant on our port side lay Songa Manara, a long low island of feathered palms and thick bush,
broken by huge coral outcrops hung with lianas and creeping
vines. Two clumps of very high and massive trees rose in the
back-ground. On our starboard was the little island of Sonya
Ya Kati and between the two lay the blue waters that were
reputed to be the swim of the man-eater.

It was necessary to get some fresh food, so we ran out the
rods and within a few minutes Anna had a heavy strike, the
fish plunging deep and then coming in on the reel after a half-
hearted fight. It turned out to be a striped Rock Cod, weighing

45 lbs. Shortly after, I caught his grandson and then in quick succession, three more of the same ilk, averaging about 5 lbs. each. There was a lull and then a tremendous strike on Anna's rod which bent almost double as the line whizzed under the boat. After playing the fish really magnificently, she topped the performance by actually landing it without the gaff, which had been broken in the struggle. Again it was a Rock Cod, all mouth and spiky fins, and it tipped the scales at a few ounces over 90 lbs. This we impaled on a shark hook and, attached to a line that had been tested at 3000 lbs, the succulent corpse drifted away into deeps waters.

The sun blazed from a cloudless sky and as we had tasted nothing cooler than warm water for the past week, we welcomed the arrival of a Songa native bearing two wild pineapples and a basket of fresh mangoes. When we mentioned the great shark, he confirmed its existence adding several details that enabled me to hazard a guess as to its precise species.

"How big is it?" I asked.

"Like that," he replied, pointing to his 30 ft. canoe. "It is a terrible fish, Bwana-Mkouba," he went on, "when it passes, it is like a dhow rushing with the wind in its sail, and it is striped like the lion of India".

The best part of the day being over we had steeled our minds against the temptation to burst headlong into the bush in search of the ruins, feeling that the project was altogether too important and that it should await the next day when, with our equipment ready and some working hours before us, we could give ourselves whole-heartedly to the task.

The afternoon crawled away in a miasma of heat, spiritually relieved by a really marvellous concert of birds amid the trees of Songa Manara.

One species gave vent to an exquisite warble while another

would chime in with a single ringing note resembling exactly the striking of a gigantic wine-glass and, in the pauses of the music, arose a voice of an obviously low-bred fellow whose contribution consisted of a series of clacks and tinkles as though he was counting his loose change. At length, with two white-headed fish eagles circling overhead and Anna's ninety-pound fish glimmering below, the whole ship fell asleep.

We awoke to a world of darkness. The stars were almost obscured by heavy banks of cloud and at one point only, where a faint luminosity gave promise of a moon to come, was the jungle discernible as a jagged black outline. Specks and patches of phosphorescence drifted past in the dark waters, but in no way comparable with the extraordinary spectacle which we had witnessed in the lagoon of the coral island. We had run out our rods from the stern and were just on the point of settling down to a comfortable bout of fishing and smoking when, from the velvet darkness of the mid-channel, there arose a sound which froze us.

It was far away, that reverberation, as though some vast body had broken surface and was plunging towards us through the water. We listened intently and the silence was so complete that I could hear a slow drip from the aft tank. Black silence and... yes, there it was again and nearer, and then again, much closer still and now we could hear an indescribable noise, between a grunt and a hiss, followed once more by the crash of water and yet again as the surface of the channel was ripped savagely apart. I can find no words to portray the impression of overwhelming malevolence conveyed by the thunderous plunges and splashes of the unseen thing which was rushing upon us through the darkness.

Grabbing a powerful torch, I turned the beam full upon the direction of its approach, and quite suddenly there appeared in the circle of light a high burst of foam like the wave of a speed boat, then a greyish flash as a huge body, at least twenty-five feet in length, turned slightly and with a roar of water plunged into the depth. The hissing noise was so loud that the comparison of a Westinghouse brake passed through my mind. The creature broke surface again in a burst of foam and, as it drew level with us, it appeared to slow and, for an instant, the thought arose whether it was contemplating an attack on the bait or on the boat! Then at tremendous speed the succession of splashes and flurries tore away into the distance. The thing had passed.

It was a trifling incident, perhaps, and yet for the first time I saw Anna frightened. I can say this because she is a woman of rare courage proven on numerous occasions by that combination of tough living conditions and very real physical danger that searches out the weak spot in a man's or woman's character and sends them scuttling for security. Even when collecting reptiles in the Cameroons, she had assisted me by handling living snakes as part of the day's work, but she would fish no more that night after the passing of the scarcely seen shape, and donned a jacket against the coldness which had crept over her. Until midnight we sat and listened and stared over the black waters while far below, the bait, untouched and ignored, gleamed like a green lantern. Personally, I have no doubt that we witnessed nothing else than the passage of the huge man-killing shark. "And when it passes, it is like a dhow rushing with the wind in its sail…"

The dry hissing grunt, which incidentally bore not the faintest resemblance to the 'blow' of a whale, does puzzle me, however, and the only explanation that I can offer is that the noise was caused by the suction of the monster's tail when plunging. Be that as it may, it was altogether horrific, and I shall long remember the tearing welter of foam rushing past us in the darkness of the narrow channel and on into the night like Death late for an appointment.

CHAPTER 9

THE DESERTED PALACE

For some way along the coral beach it was impossible to penetrate through the high roots of the Mkoko trees, but at length by clambering up an outcrop of rock, we discovered a game trail a foot or so in width winding away through a maze of tree boles, bushes and lianas interlaced into a deep greenish gloom. At one point along this trail, we came on a small clearing in which Nature had posed one of those abrupt contrasts which are her delight, for there, in the middle, stood an old tree leafless and dead and of a silvery grey and, perched all over it, their scarlet bodies and iridescent blue heads shining like scattered jewels in the sunlight, were scores of lovely long-tailed Honeybirds. They were so tame, through lack of contact with man, that we were able to approach within a few feet without disturbing them. After this, the trail grew even narrower and the bush more dense. The humidity of the forest closed in upon us with the intensity of some poisonous hot-house and we gasped and panted for breath while the sweat squelched in our boots and ran in streams from our chins and finger-tips.

At length we were reduced to using our machetes, when, suddenly, I chanced to notice, through the surrounding gloom, a dark outline which on closer examination turned out to be the crumbling remains of a great wall, such as one might find around the domain of some decayed and ruined manor house in England. We were on the right track. A few minutes later, after traversing a space of grass and bushes, we burst our way through a final maze of trees into a world of awe-inspiring unreality.

We were before the portal of a great palace.

Imagine to yourself a place the size of Hampton Court or the Tower of London, deposited in the jungle and left to rot for centuries of time. There it stood, tremendous, overwhelming, its high doorway gaping open in an arch of darkness, through which one could just discern an anteroom lined with stone benches. On every side towered crumbling walls, hewn from grey coral blocks, and windows and doorways and great pillars and arches that reared up tier upon tier from the livid colours of the jungle. It was the most subduing spectacle that I have ever seen in my life, this relic of a lost civilization.

Moving as quietly as possible, we passed through the main doorway and the anteroom with its stone benches, and so into a great square space lined with pointed arches set within corresponding rows of oblong apertures, leading in turn into a succession of rooms, each with its broken doorway and gaping liana-draped window, through which the green twilight of the jungle dimly penetrated. Dark rubbish-choked holes in the floors hinted at subterranean chambers, the depth of which defied the light of my torch. After clambering over heaps of fallen masonry and through more arches, we entered the remains of another great court, which, from the series of hollows and declivities in the floor, was probably the court of baths. At one end, high up in the wall, peeped a discreet little window, through which the Prince of the time had been pleased, doubtless, to contemplate the beauties of his women.

On we went, and on. The size of the place was simply staggering. Deep wells, half filled with débris, opened at our feet; above our heads domes split in two by the axe of time, showed their interiors decorated with delicate fluting, while

PALACE OF SONGA MANARA: ENTRANCE

PALACE OF SONGA MANARA: ONE OF THE COURTYARDS

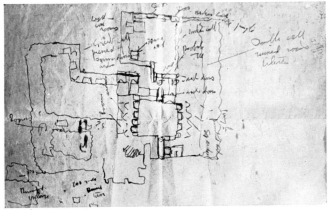

PALACE OF SONGA MANARA: ANOTHER COURTYARD

AUTHOR'S ROUGH CHART OF THE PALACE

in one domed room a number of bright blue celadon bowls were still inset in the ceiling, a style of decoration beloved by the Shirazi-Persians of a thousand years ago; and through the space once occupied by the roofs of state apartments, huge forest trees towered upwards and drooped their trailing vines over the architraves and old grey walls below. The shadows and the sunlight mingled together in a green miasma and the only sound to break the stillness was the croaking of an eagle hunched on the top of a gigantic old Baobab tree whose roots were deep in the court which once rang with the splash of water and the laughter of women.

But there were dwellers in the palace, silent dwellers who occupied their own special apartments. In a communal room lived the bats, line upon line of furry bundles which broke into life upon our entrance and flew about our heads, yet strangely enough, there was no sign of a bat in any other part of the ruin. In one court-yard we came upon a low arched doorway which led into a little chamber, dark and dank and musty, which we were on the point of entering when, observing a shadowy movement on the ground and switching on the torch, we were horrified to see that the whole floor was alive with huge six-inch centipedes, in colour black with brilliant vermilion legs and mandibles. I counted more than twenty mating pairs and in very truth was that dank closet the Bridal Chamber of nightmares.

Beyond the palace were the remains of what appeared to be watch-towers, and beyond them again a separate series of ruins which are probably those of a village which housed the less important retainers and domestics.

I can give no better idea of the size of the whole, than by the statement that despite the fact that we had pickaxes and shovels with us, there and then we gave up any idea of excavating. To excavate this fantastic place will take two years of solid work with a pick and shovel brigade of a hundred natives. Probably the results would be startling. *

The main fabric of the palace is Shirazi-Persian of the twelfth century but the foundations would appear to be far older, and there are traces of an earlier and cruder architecture encased, as it were, within the Islamic structure. When one bears in mind that Sheba's port of Salala — a port erected by her officials for the loading of the gold from Solomon's mines — lies within seventy miles, it is remotely possible that the original construction of the palace on the forgotten island of Songa Manara may have been erected for the emissaries of the greatest queen in the history of the world.

After spending the whole day in exploring that vast labyrinth of ruins, at sundown we returned to the ship and, our minds being so occupied with all that we had seen that sleep was out of the question, we curled up in the stern and fished and talked together as we watched the wonder of the tropical stars blazing in the night sky.

"I think that I can rest now," Anna said at last and began to reel in her line. As the bait, an eight-inch rock cod, broke surface, there came all in the same instant a rush of water, a sudden tearing snap and the flash of a white belly beneath the stern of the boat. It was a shark and he had taken the lot, literally hook, line and sinker. It must have been a fair size, for Anna was using big-game tackle with a breaking strain of many hundreds of pounds' weight. Thus was the close of a perfect day.

The food problem was becoming acute. For weeks past, we

* Since the completion of this book it has been announced that Dr. Gervaise Matthews, the archaeologist, has reached Songa Manara and is now engaged on large-scale excavations.

had not tasted fresh meat; fruit and greens were few and far between and the supply of fish highly speculative. So, on the next morning I set out with my rifle in search of buck and spent an abortive day following various game trails through the interior of the island. Of spoor and hoof marks there were plenty but never a sight of the bush buck. Just as the first star appeared overhead I found myself in a clearing which I recognized as being in the neighbourhood of the ruined palace, and on a sudden impulse turned my steps in that direction. I wanted to visit the place alone and in the quiet dusk. No shade of trepidation had even crossed my mind until I stood before the black silence of that gaping doorway. Then, with my foot on the threshold, I confess that I paused while all the horrors of M. R. James and Arthur Machen gibbered and mewed at me through the musty curtains of memory. I had literally to force myself to go forward.

The anteroom yawned in a tunnel of shadows through which I felt my way slowly towards the grey glimmer of light which denoted the courtyard beyond. There I seated myself on a block of fallen masonry for, and I confess it shamefacedly, I could not for the life of me go further.

All around, the doorways gaped like little black mouths and every arch was a pall of darkness, waiting... waiting... expecting... a dream or the whisper of a velvet sandal. The crumbling walls, fallen in places into shapeless masses of stone and rising in others to pinnacles, gnawed and fretted by the fangs of time, tumbled away in a grey untidiness like that of a looted vault, and the silence enwrapping the whole vast labyrinth crept over one's imagination with the murmurings and hummings that belong to the interior of a great shell rather than the deserted abodes of man. It was a fearsome place.

I tried to concentrate on the factual, to keep my thoughts

bent upon the faded splendour of the architecture and the soft transient effects of the twilight through the sightless windows. But in vain. The spectral equation was too much. Here amid these ruinous fragments, men had lived and loved, and women dreamed; hate and death and the burnings of the human heart had run their allotted spell, only to fade and crumble into the grey ashes of extinction, together with the stately palace whose pomp and luxury had fed or forced their lives. There, over there beneath the shadowed arch, were the stone benches once occupied by the throngs awaiting Audience; the mudsplashed courier sleeping in his mantle, pursy little officials then as now, begemmed swaggering captains of galleys, and suitors, above all, the suitors with anxiety at their hearts, fearing and hoping and fretting over variations of our very own fears and hopes and frets. But what had we gained in the thousand years which had passed? Improvement in drains and doctors, while the beauty of *their* creations still remained on the face of the earth to mock the ludicrous farce of a civilization which, for the first time in human history and reversing the whole process of nature, excelled in destruction over creation and, as its worst consequence, held not the sublime, the rare and the gifted, but the impure clay of common men as the lodestar for the future progress of humanity. In the Age of Slaves, the freeman had still outnumbered them, and now, in the "Age of Freedom", for the first time liberty had fled from the majority. Genius, statecraft, the very power of leadership having become suspect in a world where the one essential criterion — that of mediocrity — gives us the comfortable assurance that no leader shall possess any qualities whatsoever above our own immediate comprehension, Man has made sure that no man shall be free.

There, beyond the dim and broken archway through which

the first stars already glimmered in a purple sky, the sunlight had once smouldered upon rich heaps of silk and damask robes carelessly flung across the arms of slaves at the edge of the bathing pools and, sparkling upon the gaiety of the women, caressed their fragrant and naked loveliness into visions of bronze and milk-white alabaster; now, beneath their canopy of leaves that dripped and sweated in the stillness of the night, there remained only broken stones and forgotten lives ground together into the dust of ages; while across the very threshold once sacred to the foot of Beauty, there slithered a snake which, nosing its way among the rubble, passed with the stealth of a poisonous shadow into the recesses of the palace.

Night had fallen with its usual accompaniment of sheet lightning and, from time to time, a flicker of faint but ruddy light shot through the gaping fanes to illumine, for an instant, the walls and domes and chambers of the ancient ruin, all draped and enwrapped with lianas as with gigantic cobwebs from the Castle of the Sleeping Beauty. Slowly, I was aware of a strange tension in the atmosphere... was it mere imagination or had I overstayed my welcome?

Picking up my rifle, I felt my way between the stone benches for those who awaited Audience and so out into the darkened forest, leaving the ruined palace of Songa Manara to its phantoms and its dreams.

CHAPTER 10

DANGEROUS NEIGHBOURS

On the far tip of the island of Songa Manara arose the highpitched ratten roofs of a tiny native village, nestling under a grove of magnificent palm trees. The ground, close-cropped by goats and littered with the husks of fallen coconuts, still bore testimony, in the shape of an occasional roughly hewn stone, of that ancient mysterious civilization whose palace, like a shadow rotting in the jungle, laid its ghostly presence so heavily upon the lives of the living that none would approach within sight of its walls from twilight until dawn. With the golden-green blaze of the sun on the banana trees and the vivid blue of the sea flashing between the tall grey boles of the coconut palms, the hamlet of the Songa Manara natives was something from the pages of De Vere Stacpoole. A beach of the purest white sand rippled along the edge of a lagoon protected by an outer reef against which the rollers of the Lindi Sewa channel battered and broke in an eternal roar of surf.

This place looked promising and, armed with a casting rod and reel, I essayed my luck from the beach, slowly working my way towards a small promontory that stuck out into deeper water. From there I was able to cast towards the centre of the lagoon and the bait had scarcely reached the bottom when, without any suggestion of a strike, the rod in my hands commenced to bend. It was a slow heavy movement exactly as though a great hand had closed on the hook and was now pulling steadily in the depth of the lagoon. A big octopus, I thought, in which case it will let go as I wind in. But that was just what I could not do. I pumped hard, gained a few feet and pumped again. Then the line came in quickly for fifty yards, only to stop before a sudden tremendous pressure at the other end. This performance was repeated in a series of short winds, jerks and long sullen periods, when the creature, whatever it was, lay sulking on the bottom. Now I was gaining again and then, quite suddenly, a few yards beyond the point, the water commenced to boil furiously, and a long black whip flickered wickedly above the surface. Pumping and winding and certain that my shoulder muscles would at any moment burst into flames, I worked the thing into the shallows, where it lay with wings flapping and its daggered tail striking and smiting in every direction.

It was an Eagle Ray, a fact that warranted an exceedingly circumspect approach and, as the sunlight glinted dully on its spotted diamond-shaped back and on the twelve-inch poisoned dagger protruding half-way down its tail, horrible details of the deaths which had overtaken men who had been struck by this venomous type of creature filled my mind. Even history recorded its crimes, for had not Ulysses himself been killed by just such a fish? Choosing my moment to hurl a heavy knapsack on its tail, I sliced once with my hunting-knife, the black whip still twisting and striking flew across the sand, and a second blow severed the spinal cord.

The weapon of the Eagle Ray, used for both offensive and defensive purposes, works on very much the same principle as the fangs of a snake. The dagger itself is hollow and connects with a venom sac set in the base of the spine, with the result that, as the point of the weapon punctures the flesh of its victim, a jet of vitriolic poison is injected. The results are appalling. The flesh of the inflicted limb, as though in sympathy with the physical agony, not only inflates but loses all resilience, so that the dents caused by the grip of a hand fail to fill out again when the pressure of the fingers is removed. Death, as a rule, follows slowly, except where adequate medical treatment is immediately available; but in the case of the Eagle Ray's worse relative, the almost circular Death Ray, fatality can come within twenty seconds of the strike. Though somewhat coarse, the Eagle Ray is quite edible, and was, in this instance, a very welcome addition to our depleted cooking-pots.

But it was meat that we needed, and needed desperately. In conditions where the slightest physical effort soaked one from head to foot in a hot welter of sweat, meat alone could revitalize wasted energies. Furthermore, the great Tiger Shark was probably too old a soldier to be drawn irresistibly within range of my lines by anything less than the scent of fresh blood in the water. So, all the next day, I followed the faint marks of the bush buck through the shadowy world of the jungle and though hours were spent, hidden deep in the bushes, at the crossing of game trails, I might as well have stalked a race of ghosts. Nevertheless, though the search for food was a failure, I had occasion to use my rifle in a most unexpected way.

The game trail which I was following petered out in a wilderness of tall red-berried bushes, beyond which arose the murmur of the sea, so clean and cool and wholesome after the hot stifling sweat of my long hours in the bush that I hacked my way eagerly through the last of the undergrowth in anticipation of a short rest with a pipe and a breath of clean air.

The change from the shadowy gloom into the white-hot blast of the sunlight was so dazzling that, for a moment, it seemed that I was standing on the shore with the sea before me,

CAMP, SOUTHERN KILWA KISIWANI

ANNA AND ALI

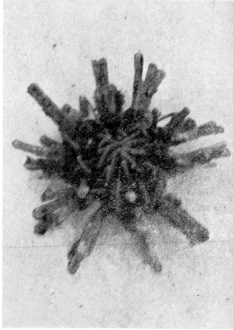

SYNAPTA (8 ft. long; photographed
through 3 ft. of water

HORNED TRUNK FISH *(top)*

SEA URCHIN

when, in fact, I was on a rocky escarpment, fifty feet above the sand. The descent was hard and, being much too lazy to attempt it, having chosen a shady spot I settled down gratefully and prepared to relax. Idly, my eyes followed the contours of the ridge with its apron of white coral sand, glaring at one moment in the sunlight and cooling the next under a flood of green crystal. On looking further still, however, I forgot all about lighting my pipe.

There, three hundred yards away to the left, in the mouth of what appeared to be a creek running across the sand into the sea, lay a huge shark!

The water was so shallow that I could see the brute's white belly resting on the bottom, while not only the dorsal but its whole back jutted above the surface with the high caudal fin of the tail waving lazily in the dancing heat waves that shimmered over the water. It was not the Tiger shark, however, but a Blue Pointer of at least fifteen feet in length, a type of Maneater only less dangerous than the Tiger and White sharks.

Swiftly I surveyed the situation. The undergrowth on the top of the ridge was so dense that it would have been a martyrdom to attempt it, while if I descended the fifty foot drop, my sudden appearance on the shore might arouse the brute's suspicions and send him wriggling back into his proper domain of deep water. Knowing the habits of sharks, habits which are in complete contradiction to the dangerously ignorant claptrap which has attempted, in recent times, to whitewash these fearless killers as bundles of nerves easily driven off by splashing and shouting, I was determined to kill him by the one means which I had at my disposal and so, drawing a careful sight with the .375 Mannlicher, I pressed the trigger. The result was as appalling as it was unexpected.

7

A wave of water shot into the air as the stricken shark reared upwards, its great tail lashing volley after volley of spray over the beach as it rolled into deeper water. An instant later the disturbance increased tenfold as several sleekly-moving triangles, springing from nowhere, closed in on the mortally wounded killer. Through a maelstrom of foam and flying spume, I had occasional glimpses of a bluish-tinted body rolling and twisting in a flurry of sharks' fins; and then, quite suddenly, the sea was so calm and serene and utterly at peace that one might have considered the whole incident as a trick of the imagination, were it not for the fact that the foam floating like a fringe of lace on the water's edge was white no longer but stained with a lovely rose-pink.

Scrambling down to the beach, I ran along the sand and into the shallows on the chance that the great head might be procurable yet as a trophy but, though I was standing in no more than two feet of water, I was already under surveillance. A few yards farther out, two grey dorsal fins rising suddenly above the surface, commenced a slow patrol up and down, up and down, with the precision of two hellish sentries. They were still there when, having re-ascended the crags, I took a last glance shorewards before commencing to tunnel my way painfully back again into the green matted wall of the bush on my return journey to the ship.

I awoke early and crawling out of my sleeping bag, tiptoed along to the fishing chair in the stern. The ship was wrapped in slumber, and over sea and sky and coral isle there brooded that condition of absolute stillness which falls like a pall during the few brief minutes that separate the tropic night from the tropic dawn. It was the swoon of nature when all the myriad colours and outlines which compose the fabric of the living earth fuse and melt together into a dream world of misty

lavender so nebulous and delicate that the very rocks themselves seemed moulded into a sudden aerial transparency
above a shore of mother-of-pearl.

In the east the whole arch of the heavens glowed and trembled
in a luminous purple radiance like the sheen of hidden fires
in the heart of a vast amethyst. Slowly, almost imperceptibly,
a pink blush stole up the sky, warmed into a wonderful arch of
rose-coloured light and then, with a sudden almost bewildering
rapidity, spread and brightened into an infinity of the palest gold flecked with tiny whorls and veins of scintillating
flame. There was a moment of ecstasy, silent, immobile, glorious and then the edge of a blazing white-hot disc pierced the
violet line of the ocean and a new day was born.

Nature awoke. The woods of Songa Manara burst once
more into song while the white egrets fluttered down on the
long empty shore like a rain of snowdrops. A short distance
from the ship the water commenced to boil and flash in sudden
wild gleams of blue and silver as a school of breakfast-hungry
Kingfish got to grips with the menu. I was watching the bursts
of spray speckled with the dark blobs of wretched Skip-jacks
leaping for their lives, when a long reddish-brown back appeared for a moment and sank slowly from sight. Even in that short
glimpse, it had struck me as curious, in some way unusual. The
movement was rather like that of an indolent porpoise, and yet
there was something lacking... why, of course, it had no dorsal
fin! Shark, porpoise, small whale, swordfish, all dorsal fins,
jewfish, manatee... *Manatee,* that strange creature with the
breasts of a woman, the mermaid of the legends..., I rushed to
the side just in time to catch a perfect view of the queer ungainly mammal swimming past the stern of the ship. Its glistening back shone with an almost reddish colour in the clear
water and I got a fleeting impression of looking down on a

frightful eight-foot long caricature of a woman with a huge neckless head at one end and a tail at the other. A moment later and it was no more than a dim shape sinking down, down, down into the purple depth far below.

It is curious that the Manatee, though composed of very rich red flesh, is seldom if ever attacked by shark or barracouda. Among the greedy meat-eaters of the ocean, this helpless succulent creature is taboo. Man alone, the greatest scavenger of all, stoops to eat it, though often with the horrible proviso that the fisherman take oath that he has not indulged in sexual intercourse with the Manatee.

The perennial reek of fried fish wafted along the deck.

"Breakfast's ready," called Anna, appearing in the hatchway with a huge beer mug full of tea.

"Fish again?" I groaned.

"What else? Not a high price for Freedom! One free fish, the trophy of blood, sweat and tears versus tenpence worth of meat and that glorious charter of human liberty, the ration book. Take your choice."

"You are far too literal," I observed. "Do you realise, woman, that I had to shave this morning in the residue of yesterday's tea?"

She laughed unfeelingly.

"The tannin will suit your sunburn. And isn't it all worth while? No horrible little officials and regulations and designs for life cut out for us by nail scissors in Whitehall. I'd rather see you shaving in cold tea for the rest of your days than splashing about in the planned tapwater of the planned existence."

"Well, we feel the same way about it, otherwise we wouldn't be here at all," I smiled. "And now what about a swim?"

"Later on, perhaps, but I must de-tick Jum-Jum before I do

anything else. Don't wait for me but do be careful where you walk..."

"...Because of Stone fish," I finished for her.

"And not to..."

"...go out of my depths because of shark," I called out in mock innocence and only avoided the well-aimed remains of a mango by leaping into the dinghy.

I ran along the white beach for a few hundred yards until I reached a spot where the sandy bottom sloped very gradually through the shallow water for, though I had joked about it, I was well aware that to swim in deep water in the Songa Manara channel was an invitation to a most unpleasing form of death. The full blast of the sun was turning the coral sand into a furnace, and throwing off my only garment, a native cloth skirt called a Shuka, I stretched my bare limbs in a lazy sensuous animal freedom before flopping into the cool paradise that splashed and sparkled at my feet. Bathing shorts, in common with a great many other things, belonged to a dim and very stupid world a million miles away.

Holding my breath, I lay on my face in the water and watched the white sand ripples and tiny brilliant shells within six inches of my nose while the hot tingle of the sunlight ran up and down my back like a caress. Then I wallowed and rolled and splashed in the cool green ecstasy of it all, and finally floated for minutes or hours or was it days while the dome of the heavens beat overhead with a glare like polished brass and the pods of a red flowering tree, whose branches stretched towards the water's edge, bursting with tiny crackling sounds spattered seeds like drops of black blood over the coral sand.

I collected my senses and was wading only knee-deep towards the shore when I felt something flick across my right foot. It was a quick, gossamer touch like the kiss of a tiny whiplash followed instantly by a burning point of fire as though a lighted cigarette was sinking into the side of my foot. In two bounds I had reached the shore and was running towards the ship for my very life. My brain throbbed with one continuous repetition... I have been hit by a Ray... if it was a big one, then I'm a dead man... If it was a young'un, then I don't know... Never thought I could run so fast.

The ship at last, and I glanced at my foot. The right side was fiery red and horribly swollen.

"Anna," I called.

She came out of the shadowy hatchway into the blaze of the sun, radiant, lovely. "Hullo darling. Did you enjoy... My God, what's the matter!"

"Everything's all right, but we must work quickly," I said. "I have been hit by a Ray."

She went white.

"Adult?" she whispered.

"I don't know. Almost certainly not. Otherwise, already..."

"Lie on the deck. Don't move."

She was in to the cabin like a flash and back again with a candle, a box of matches and a sharp knife. She lit the candle and held the blade in the cleansing flame. She was marvellously cool now and a noticed that her hands did not tremble.

"Just a tiny cut," she said.

"Hell! This is going to be worse than the Ray!"

She gripped my foot but it was so numb and swollen that I could not even feel the pressure of her fingers. My Irish gift for anticipation shied like a horse, and looking up at the sky I fixed my mind with a horrible concentration upon the all important question whether or not our faithful Arab servant-cum-man-at-arms, Hassan, was using the right type of oil on our medieval armour now housed in Morocco.

"Look," said Anna, suddenly.

I did so reluctantly and then with considerable interest. She had opened a small slit in the side of my foot and was squeezing manfully but instead of blood a clear substance like the white of an egg welled sullenly from the wound and dripped upon the deck. Slowly the white turned to pink and at last came the blood.

"There!" she said.

I lay very still while an overwhelming urge for sleep crept over me. I closed my eyes. There was a period of rather tangled peace and then... throb... throb... throb. When I opened my eyes again I found Anna still watching me, her face cupped in her hands.

"How much time has passed?" I asked.

"An hour."

"Then it was only a young 'un, thank God. But you'll have to cut again."

She nodded bravely, and the performance was repeated. The white poison streamed from the wound, spurted, dribbled and then the blood flowed strong and red.

"I think that's the end of it," I remarked as she deftly bandaged the gash.

"Please heaven!" And she vanished into the cabin. A moment later came the welcome rattle of the old tea kettle.

CHAPTER 11

INTERIM

We did everything in our power during the following two days to get the man-eater, but all in vain. We moved out to his favourite swim around the island of Sonya Ya Kati keeping a sharp look-out while the vast Rock Cod slowly became putrid and scared every fish in the vicinity. On our last night before returning across the channel to Songa Manara, I sat up until dawn, on watch over a sea of oiled silk spangled with the clear-cut brilliant reflections of the stars, and in the early hours of the morning there came a curiosity which well repaid my vigil.

Far away on the water there appeared a faint luminescence which, approaching by very slow degrees, took on the semblance of some vast sea-serpent of green light. As it drifted past the *Gloria Scott*, it seemed to be about 70 feet long, twice the length of my boat, and about 10 feet wide, and was composed of nothing more deadly than a solid mass of phosphorescent fish spawn. Nevertheless, it was an interesting spectacle, blazing away in the darkness of the night.

We moved into the main channel of Lindi Sewa to continue our efforts after the Tiger shark but it was antelope meat and blood which were needed to summon him from his lair and these were the very things that we had not got. Anna replenished our larder with five Blue Spotted Rock Cod, beautiful creatures of a brilliant orange red splashed with turquoise blue.

My foot had mended well and so once again I was relegated

to the thankless task of trying to get some fresh meat. Accompanied by Ali and Mravile and two rifles, I landed on the southernmost tip of Kilwa Kisiwani where on the previous day I had noticed through my binoculars a bush buck licking the salt deposit on the coral spurs exposed by the fall of the tide. I must confess that the realisation that I was almost certainly the first white man to penetrate inland from that end of the island gave me the thrill of a schoolboy. We forced our way through a thick barrier of Mkoko trees, the roots of which rose directly from the salt water like a tangled mass of spider's legs, and found ourselves not on solid ground as we had fondly imagined but on the verge of a hidden inner lagoon stretching for a mile in front of us. There was no alternative but to cross it, and so forth we set in single file and up to our thighs in water.

The scene was iridescently lovely, the jungle-covered banks all shimmering and quivering in the sunlight while across the smooth surface of the lagoon a line of pink flamingoes stretched away into the distance like an avenue of rose-quartz statues. Cranes and herons paused to survey us gravely and then returned to the more important matter of probing for crabs and shellfish. On our approach to the opposite shore, we were confronted by my old friend the Blow Fish, that curious creature which has the power, when frightened or excited, of inflating itself into a ball bristling with spikes. This little fellow, striped in gold and black, was so furious at our invasion of his territory that coming up to the surface he inflated to the size of a football until, having overdone it and lost all control of his equilibrium, he had perforce to turn two slow back-summersaults, his small fins and tail vibrating like fans in his efforts to prevent this loss of dignity; then shooting out a jet of water, he suddenly deflated into a very insignificant little fish and scurried away into the sea-grass.

The day sweated past with no success and much dolour. For miles we trudged along blistering coral beaches and over tidal estuaries the pools of which were so hot that it was actually painful to wade through them; we crept into caves which probably had never been entered by man and were rewarded for our curiosity by bat droppings and bumped pates. Plunging into the bush, we were seized on by wait-a-bit thorns, our hats whipped from our heads while our singlets were rent and half-torn from our backs; a snake-like liana got to mating grips with my rifle, and my left shoe was dragged off and firmly embedded in the maw of a startlingly intelligent-looking thorn bush. My Africans were in no better state than their master, and at last by a sort of unspoken telepathy we turned as one man and whipped, torn and bedraggled, crashed our way desperately back to the red-hot beach. Over our return journey I prefer to draw a veil.

But there was a reward, a reward of sensual delight beside which the pleasures of the most accomplished boudoir fall into comparative insignificance. I refer to the fact that arriving back at our starting point, I was able to sit on the root of a Mkoko tree and, dabbling my feet in the sea, allow a stream of warm liquid from my water bottle to trickle slowly down my throat. The sensations were marvellous beyond belief and I strongly recommend the whole performance to the tired voluptuary.

The evenings were very quiet and very wonderful. Sculling ashore in the dinghy with our battered old gramophone and an assortment of whispery Italian love songs, we would settle down in some snug corner among the mango roots. Above and behind us, the loom of almost impenetrable bush hung like a black curtain pierced by jagged rents ablaze with stars and the only sounds, emphasizing rather than disturbing the immense silence, were the sharp click-clack click-clack of mud-crabs and the soft silky rustling of strange little Lung-fish creeping from the sea and up into the branches of the trees. The darkness shimmered with fireflies blinking and winking in long lazy swoops of green flame so perfect in grace that it seemed as though, on hearing Tchaikovsky's music among the mango roots, the lights of the night freely gave up their souls to become for one short magic hour the luminous ghosts of his waltzing flowers. In the spell of a tropic shore, murmuring with primeval noises, a man loses his grip on reality, on life, on a whole world and, leaning his head on a woman's breast, he is content merely to lie and dream and listen in the shadows and the broken starlight.

It would be quite unfair to leave the south of Kilwa Kisiwani without some reference to the crabs, and I should be very glad to hear from some zoologist more knowledgeable on the subject than myself whether or not the following brief descriptions suggest any rare form of crustacea. There were three particular types that I saw in the Kilwa lagoon and which personally I have seen in no other part of Africa. One was a crab which I found in a hole in a Mkoko tree. It was black all over and its shell was square, while each segment of the legs was covered with a square plate, so that the whole creature looked as though it were composed of a series of black cubes; another species was an olive crescent-shaped crustacea, the front of the shell being attached to the claws with the result that, when the claws were folded in, the crab became to all appearances an inanimate oblong sea-shell; the third was the most curious of all and when I first saw the thing I thought that it was a tumbleweed blowing lightly along the shore. On closer examination, however, it turned out to be a large jade-coloured crab of gossamer lightness, very high in the leg and with yellow eyes standing straight up from the shell like a pair of twin peri-scopes. The pupils of the eyes were feline in shape but vertical.

My general impression of the terrain in those parts may be summed up in shortage of sharks and other big fish but richly endowed with smaller forms of life, some endemic and perhaps even unknown.

We passed a further two days in fishing and studying through the water-glass the huge, mushroom-shaped Brain-head corals around which centred, in brilliant enamelled colours, the communal life of the sea.

Then we held a conference in the cabin. If we were to get to close grips with big fish then we must do so before the change of the monsoon. The Mafia Channel with its myriad islets and inlets seemed to offer the greatest possibilities, and with the charts on the table before us we made our plans. First, we should go to Songo Songo, then to Okusa, a deserted island some distance byond Songo Songo, and then to Mafia itself. From there, should the big fish fail to come up to expectations, we would try to get over the niggerhead coral spires barring the passage from Mafia to the island of Chole and, once there, explore the local waters on the edge of the great Eastern Bar-rier. In the meantime it was urgently necessary that we get back to some contact point with semi-civilisation as quickly as possible, for we were down to a few gallons of drinking water and engine kerosene. So, a few days after our tussle with the thorn trees, we headed out through the reefs and along the coast towards Kilwa Masoko.

We were running parallel with the outer reef of Kilwa Kisi-wani Island when at some distance ahead the surface of the sea was suddenly agitated by a series of swirls and eddies in the midst of which there arose several dark pointed objects resembling dorsal fins. Our first impression that we were approaching a school of sharks proved wrong when, for an instant, a long flat shape broke surface in a flurry of spray, curled up its extremities into two snow-white sails that were almost dazzling against the blue water, and sank slowly from view.

Crouching on the harpoon platform, I loosened the twelve-foot shafts from their lashings while the great bat-like shapes continued to rise and fall through the glass-clear depth a hundred yards in front of our bows. The engine was throttled back and gradually we drifted down upon them as with every muscle tensed I awaited the moment to strike.

The minutes ticked away. With a curious feeling of detachment, I watched the little feather of foam curling around the prow. A delicate mauve jelly fish floated by, and then far down in the depth, almost directly beneath the platform, a great dark shadow commenced to rise like the top of a lift coming up from the bed of the sea. A second shadow joined it, and together they rushed for the surface, circling around and around each other in spirals of sheer delight, flitting and flirting higher and ever higher through the liquid sapphire until with a crash of spray that fountained over the harpoon platform the sea was rent asunder and the two Mantas were flaunting their wings in the glory of the sun. There they lay, gambolling with the grace of swallows, their chocolate-coloured backs and the brilliant white of their undersides forming a slow minuet of colour as the weird creatures circled and curvetted beneath the bows of the ship. They were not large specimens, no more than fifteen feet across, and spiralling lazily on the blue of the sea, they bore an extraordinary resemblance to monstrous marine bats. I rested on the shaft of my harpoon and watched them in their love-dance. It was no use; I could not kill them. Harmless creatures, the destruction of any specimens under thirty feet across would be murder. A great bull

Manta, fully capable of towing the ship and turning on any small boat which offered annoyance, such a creature as that would be something for honourable advancement, but as far as my harpoons were concerned these half-grown lovers should remain in peace. Slowly we drew away and the last we saw of them was the tip of a wing curling above a high line of foam that tossed and sparkled in our wake.

On reaching Kilwa Masoko we found that the M. V. *Mombasa* had just arrived in the Estuary and within an hour one of the officers boarded the *Gloria Scott*.

"The Captain's compliments. If you or Mrs. Conan Doyle would care to have a fresh bath..."

His words were lost in our rush over the side.

CHAPTER 12

MRINI

There was a warning, and it came to pass. Some places, in common with certain human beings, seem to emanate a positive vibration of misfortune, and so far as we were concerned the wretched hamlet of Kilwa Masoko was a typical case in point. On our previous visit we had been laid by the heels through engine trouble and now, hoping to be away within twenty-four hours en route to the Mafia Channel, we had no sooner arrived in Kilwa than the engine packed up on the spot. Grimly we had commenced repairs when the tug *Thekia* arrived in the estuary on one of her rare visits, towing a lighter for the loading of tropical nuts, and we had a happy chance temporarily to forget our problems during a most enjoyable evening which we spent on board the *Thekia* as the guests of Captain Bayley and his officers. Dinner over, conversation turned to storms and sea life and fishing during which the Captain gave a graphic account of the *Thekia's* recent encounter with a Whale shark within a hundred miles of Kilwa. This was exciting news, for the Whale shark is not only the largest of all fish but a comparative rarity and, though we ourselves were not destined to see the fish, it remained along the coast and a month later gave the crew of a small copra schooner the fright of their lives when, amid the crash of opening seas, white-spotted greenish leviathan nearly twice the length of their schooner rose alongside and commenced to rub its great flanks against the ship.

Mr. Robinson, the First Officer of the *Thekia*, raised his

eyebrows significantly over our intention to operate in the
Mafia waters at this time of the year and, not content with a
few words of warning across the dinner table, he had the very
real kindness to send me a letter on the subject by the hand of a
native on the following morning.

His message was to warn me that in view of the smallness
of our boat, we should be prepared night and day to deal with
an immediate danger which was likely to arise under the local
conditions during the months of January and February.
During that period the prevailing N. E. Monsoon would
be blowing fairly regularly, under the guise of a wind called the
Kaskazi, but the real menace lay in the fact that without warning out of a perfectly clear sky there might arise a hurricane in
miniature, blowing always from the West, and thus contrary to
the prevailing wind. This Mrini as it is called rarely lasted more
than an hour but, even in that space of time, it was capable
of raising such a sea as would drag an anchor and in the case
of our little *Gloria Scott* must represent a very real and direct
menace. If we were to fish and explore the Mafia, then it
would be absolutely necessary to find an almost land-locked
base wherein we could anchor by night safely ensconced
against this javelin from the heavens.

I made a careful note of all this but as we felt that there
would be no immediate danger in the Kilwa estuary, despite
the fact that we were both engine-less and sail-less, we shelved
the matter in the spirit of 'that time that worry'.

A few nights after the departure of the *Thekia* a Mrini
swept suddenly across the estuary to the accompaniment of
thunder and lightning and though the helpless boat pitched
and rolled violently, the anchor held and the whole thing was
over in twenty minutes. Like fools, we did not take any extra
precautions on the strength of this experience, and yet it is

CORAL ISLE

A.C.D. ON WHITE DEATH SHARK

difficult to say what these could have been short of actually beaching the boat.

The very next evening, the sun went down in a wonderful glow of rose-coloured light which continued long after the disappearance of the flaming orb to embue with a loveliness almost ethereal the gaps and crevices in a mass of cloud which, looming along the whole western horizon, bathed sea and land in a pale grey light. Every few moments, now here, now there, this wall of cloud was torn by successive flashes and glares of lightning which, confining itself to the interior of the cumuli, and playing with almost incredible rapidity, suggested that some celestial incendiary, armed with a lamp and crouching to his work, was hurrying to and fro within towers and battlements of alabaster. Occasionally, through the interstices of the cloud and in sharp contrast to the steady play of the sheet lightning, a fork of dazzling orange fire would shoot from sky to earth with the speed and malice of a dagger stroke. Yet, despite the tempest which apparently raged internally, this grey wall grew neither larger nor smaller but enwrapped the whole western skyline in an awful majesty and stillness. There was nothing to be done but to hope for the best and go to sleep under conditions that were rather more comfortable than usual for, for some reason best known to themselves, the mosquitos had completely vanished.

It was 2 a.m. when we were awoken by a low moaning which increased with such velocity that by the time I had pulled on my shorts and dashed from the wheel-house, the wind had risen to a shriek which almost drowned the cries and shouts of the crew as they scrambled from the fo'c'sle hatch and, rivalling the peals of thunder overhead, turned the darkness into one great holocaust of rage and uproar. Sheet after sheet of lightning tore across the heavens, conveying in a stark

8

violet glare fleeting glimpses of the water rising and already tormented into swirls of foam and spray which, smashing against our sides, caused the little ship to add the groaning of her timbers to the mightier voices of the night.

Then came the rain. It was a solid deluge that swept all before it. The wind was rising, and the ship straining at her mooring. The hurricane lamps were blown out, and chilled to the marrow by the freezing blast of the rain, we worked desperately to let out more anchor chain by the dim glimmer of a flash light, unpleasantly assisted by the blaze of lightning that every few seconds the sky rent. The yells of the crew and the pistol-shot cracking of the canvas covers over the open sides of the wheel-house added to a pandemonium that was all the more dreadful that it followed immediately on the heels of sleep.

The real dangers of our situation lay in the fact that at a hundred yards distance from our stern a lofty iron jetty, a relic of the German occupation of pre-1914, jutted far out from the shore while, at a short way beyond our bows, a bristle of upright iron girders, protruding above the surface, denoted the ruins of an even older jetty which, owing to the culpable negligence of the local authorities, had been permitted to remain.

Through the open back of the wheel-house the rain and spray drove in almost horizontally as Anna and I clung to the sides as best we could, while the gallant little ship shook and trembled like a living creature as wave after wave swept past or sent a cascade of foam hissing over the stern. The Mrini had risen with such suddenness that the phosphorescence natural to these waters had not been dispersed by preliminary stages, with the result that as every waver raced upon us from out of the darkness not only was its crest luminous but those that had already broken thundered past like tumbling masses of fire, a resemblance heightened by the hissing sound accompanying their passage and by the myriad twinkles and sparks of phosphorescent light which the violence of the rain struck from the surface of the raging waters.

An hour had staggered past but instead of abating the Mrini seemed to have increased, and it was shortly after 3 a.m. that a series of sickening lurches and the shouts of the crew rising anew above the wind warned us that the anchor had dragged and, wallowing helpless, we were at the mercy of the elements. There was nothing more to be done, so tucking Jum-Jum under my feet, Anna and I put our arms around each other and waited the event. I remember the thoughts that kept turning in my mind — we've lost control, we'll go through the mouth of the estuary and into that frightful sea and then... the reef and the end. My God, why on earth did I ever bring Anna on such a tiny boat into a hellish place like this? Will we rush through the old pier or have the whole bloody lot down on top of us?

Nearer we drove and nearer and yet, so slowly, or such it seemed at the time. In the brilliant clarity of every lightning flash I could see the gaunt shape of the old German pier growing closer and bigger and clearer until every angle of its crazy timbers and girders were imprinted on my brain. Then there came a long period of darkness and hissing water and a helter of rain that plastered our hair over our faces. There was the sound of rushing foam and when at long last the lightning blazed again we beheld the pier looming almost above our heads.

"We are in God's hands," said a voice which I did not even recognise as my own. Anna hid her face against my shoulder.

With the spray leaping half-way up the pylons, for a moment we seemed to hover upon the surge of a great wave. Then we were two yards away, then three, then ten, driving hard in the opposite direction. At the very instant, when our fate lay in the balance the wind had shifted! Words failed us in a prayer of thankfulness in the midst of that hell of darkness and wind and white water. But our danger was not over as was only too quickly apparent. We reeled along parallel with the shore, driving and rolling before the lift of the waves until in direct line with our bows and only thirty yards away, we saw jutting up through the foam of the breakers a cluster of wicked black fangs.

"The iron pylons of the ruined jetty," thought I. "There's no missing this time!"

Suddenly a tremendous bump shook the whole ship followed by another and another. Our keel had grounded.

Horrible as the feeling was, under the circumstances it was the very best thing that could have happened. Crew and all we gathered in the tiny wheel-house with its open back and a sorry lot we looked, almost naked, glistening with rain and spray and shaking in every limb with cold and reaction. And so the minutes dragged on for another endless hour, while our gallant little ship, groaning in every timber, rolled and bumped and dug in ever deeper despite the broken water that roared past, now luminious green in the darkness, now mauve under the livid brilliance of the lightning.

But surely the wind and the rain were slackening at long last. Peering outside, we thought we could discern amid the cloud wrack tearing overhead the faintest glimmer of a coming dawn.

"I heard something," I croaked. "Listen, for Christ's sake!"

We strained our ears in a sudden lull of the wind. Then we all heard it. From far inland there came surprisingly the faint crowing of a cock. The Nahoda spoke a few words in Arabic and slipped away for'ard.

"What did he say?" I demanded.

"The Nahoda said, Sah, that he is going to say his prayers," replied Ali.

And I think that as the dear old man for'ard on the harpoon platform bent his head and hands humbly towards Allah, so did all our hearts, Christian and Mahommedan alike, join with his in thankfulness to Him who had vouchsafed His Mercy to the helpless ants on the matchbox.

It will give some idea of the force of this hurricane in miniature that the District Commissioner, whose house lay a mile away, told me, when we met on the following day, that his first intimation of the storm was the sudden arrival of his heavy Persian rugs into the mosquito netting over his bed. The force of the wind, merely through the open window, had plucked them from the floor like so many pieces of paper.

CHAPTER 13

LIONS AND FIREFLIES

Kilwa Masoko is a hot hamlet of sweat and thorns and bush melting into one great virgin wilderness that, rolling away into remote distances, averages perhaps one white man every hundred miles. We filled in the time that was not devoted to working on the ship's engine by hunting after game through this bushland but, though the spoor was plentiful, I have never known an uncivilized part of Africa where buck was so difficult to come by. All day, one could wander quietly through patches of thick bush and long gentle swards of greenery broken by clumps of fine trees like a breadth of English parkland or over open spaces covered with a yellow flowering shrub intermingled with thorn bushes and waist-high elephant grass. Here and there strips of sandy earth shone golden in the surrounding green and provided ample evidence that this silent bush world was in reality thickly populated with many and divers kinds of inhabitants. The trotter marks of the wild pig crossed the delicate spoor of tiny gazelles or were almost obliterated by the larger marks of sable antelope and eland and, while passing through the long grass, it was necessary to keep alert for sudden yawning holes caused by the mining activities of ant-bears. Wart-hog were in abundance and, on one occasion, on rounding a lightning-split Baobab tree I found myself face to face with a lone boar Wart-hog, probably a rogue, which was considerably larger than any other specimen that I had seen throughout Africa. The vast beast was not in the least disturbed by this sudden encounter but stood at gaze, its ivory tusks gleaming in the sun and its tail erect like a tufted baton while it bent upon me a malevolent and piggy eye until I had passed on my way.

One evening when returning to the ship after a safari of some miles after guinea-fowl and armed only with a light shotgun, I was trudging along the bed of a dried creek and happily congratulating myself on discovering an easier route than forcing a passage through the bush, when I noticed a number of footmarks that had been freshly made on the sandy surface. As I straightened up, the stillness of the countryside seemed to take on a new and sinister quality. For the footmarks were those of four lions, three adults and a young one!

I pushed on, with many a backward glance, through the high grass and up long weary ridges of scrub bush and down shadowy dells where the vegetation met overhead in tunnels of silence and gloom, but by the time that the brief twilight had deepened into night, I was still a mile or more from the ship. I must confess that I felt not the slightest inclination to saunter along whistling with my hands in my pockets, and it took me all my time to check a continual impulse to look over my shoulder as I felt my way through the darkness and across open spaces, grey in the starlight, where every stump and shrub was a thing that crouched and held its breath.

Once I stopped to listen, and the croaking of a thousand frogs and the high-pitched screaming of the night crickets rose up at me in a wave of sound. Shaking my head to regain a sense of oral proportion, I listened again; the frogs and the crickets and... yes, something crashing through the bush! The sounds died away and assuring myself that it was only a buck, I pushed on.

By now, night had set in and the darkness of the jungle was flickering and gleaming like a witches' revel with a wild dither of fireflies, a spectacle so wonderful to behold that for the moment it swept away all other emotions. The countless drops of light drifting and circling in the air and hanging from the vegetation as though every leaf was tipped with a glowing emerald conveyed a comforting sense of companionship, though based on nothing more solid than the elements of light and movement.

Crossing another sandy delta, I made my way down a long tunnel of interlocked branches, only to end in an impasse of thorns that rent my clothes and flesh as I struggled in vain to force a passage, heartily cursing the gazelle into whose run I had blundered. I felt my way back again and then on to the right of a dark loom of trees; but surely it should be to the left and then straight on down a long clearing; and, damn it, there *was* no clearing but only an anthill like a huge stalagmite of silver against the gloom! It was then that I realized I was 'bushed' and that at night, and in the vicinity of four lions. Strangely enough the thought of blundering on and on and on into the vast hinterland, perhaps in hopeless circles, was more nerve-racking to me than the big cats. I was utterly lost and because of that fact I knew that I had to keep a tight grip on myself or yield to the temptation to rush headlong through the darkness on the wild chance that I might find my bearings before the lions found me. The only sensible thing to do was to try; so by moving first in one direction and then in another, my eyes dizzy with the swirling and whirling of the fireflies, I zigzagged about the forest and eventually picked up a far-off murmur that sounded like the sea in the Mkoko trees. I was wearily ploughing my way in what I hoped to be the right direction through grass that reached up to my shoulders when at a long distance away I caught the faint gleam of lanterns moving through the darkness of the bush. I yelled with all my might, and my heart jumped with relief as a chorus of voices raised an answering shout.

A few minutes later we had all met together in a ring of light and I was listening to the eloquent recriminations of Anna who, in view of my non-return at nightfall, had gallant-ly set out into the bush with Ali and Mravile in search of the missing body.

After we had completed our return journey to the ship and eaten a supper of bully beef and succulent ship-made scones, Jum-Jum thrust up his flat face and suggested that *he* would like a walk, so putting him in the dinghy we took him ashore and up the little sloping hill towards the native village a hun-dred yards away.

Usually this place was alive with chattering voices and moving lights but now everything was strangely tense and still. Though chinks of fire-light peeped through the palm-leaf walls of the huts, there was not a sound from the inhabitants nor a sign of anybody on the road which, edged by the black fringe of the bush, stretched away empty and desolate under the starlight. We were within a few yards of the top of the slope and the nearest hut when from out of the darkness there came a coughing grunt. We froze on the spot.

Horrible and gutteral and full of a stealthy malevolence, the chunting of a lion once heard is not easily forgotten. In one sweep gathering up fat Jum-Jum as if he were made of thistle-down, we made our way down the hill at a remarkable speed, thrust him into the dinghy and pushed off for the safety of the ship.

Then, taking my rifle, I made my way back to the shore and up the hill as warily as possible. I have seldom felt less at home, while the night took on the proportions of an enormous lion and I of one very small piece of meat. I reached the top of the slope and peered into the surrounding gloom.

Two green eyes glared at me balefully from beneath the shadow of a native hut and I could see the vague outline of a crouching body. I was looking down the sights of my rifle and was on the point of firing, when I suddenly realized that immediately beyond the lion there were tiny chinks of light peeping through the walls of the hut.

The position was extremely ticklish for, if I missed that vague shadow, the crash of the soft-nosed bullet into the hut would be almost certainly followed by the dying howl of somebody's grandmother. The lion settled the problem for at that moment with a single lithe movement he melted back into the bush. I waited only long enough to retreat without too much loss of honour and then made my way back to the shore and the safety of the eighty feet of comfortable water that separated my couch from the skulking King of Beasts.

As one wandered about this illimitable countryside, particularly over the vast deserted spaces of the upper grassland with its numerous waterholes and flowering trees and rolling oceans of rich green grass which needs but cultivation to offer peace and life to a whole continent of people, it was impossible to avoid the thought of the absolute and wanton madness of mankind or rather of the leaders and governments of mankind. In a world still richly endowed with plenty of space and natural but utterly neglected wealth, they permit their charges, the human race, to concentrate in those portions of the earth which, though once the centres of grace and culture and learning, have become the miserable cockpits of avarice, of fear and of absurd racial and class hatreds through no other fundamental cause than that of over-population.

In four out of the five continents lie vast stretches of unreclaimed land, richly endowed with everything that could

make for the well-being and security of man, and yet, for such
is our innate knavery before the generosity of our Creator, we
are incapable of taking advantage of the treasures placed at our
free disposal but continue to jostle each other in our over-
crowded corners with smaller concern for a whole world and
less of human dignity than the ant bestows on his cone of sand
or in the instinctive responsibility that prompts his living and
his dying.

But the time will surely come when, if it is to survive at all,
the human race must creep forth from the communal lunacy
of controls that confer no benefit, of excessive taxes that are
governmental plunder and all the other characteristics of a
period which is no longer the Age of Steel but, with universal
death at the mercy of science, has become instead the Age of
Buttons; and having blown up the nursery with atomic, hy-
drogenic and bacteriological toys, the remnant will at last remember that beyond the stench of human sweat and the in-
dignity of man, neglected and far away, are high green places
and valleys quiet and dreaming where the blue waterlilies float
unpicked upon their amber pools.

Stranded as we were and our work disastrously delayed, I
cannot pretend that we enjoyed ourselves nor lacked physical
evidence of our enforced sojourn. We had lost weight not only
through the lack of proper food supplies but owing to continuously broken nights caused by insects. Save on the occasions
when we were blest by a wind, the lighting of our lanterns was
the signal every evening for a vast onslaught of mosquitos,
brown-bodied sausage flies, flying ants, cockroaches armed like
the pard and of greyhound speed, and horrific-looking Praying
Mantii, some of the latter being more than six inches in length.
The insect legions, hustling aboard in their thousands, demon-
strated not only their hunger but a power of harikari that put

to shame the Japanese, and by the light of lamps piled with roasting bodies we learnt the stoic necessity of drinking our coffee at an average of eighteen mosquitos and a flying ant per gulp. On the bookshelf a huge black and yellow hornet commenced the building of an earth and spittle nest supported on one side by *Guy Mannering* and on the other by *Count Robert of Paris*. Worms were busy with the ship's bottom, and the general activity was enlivened by music of an ever-lasting and maddening symphony of clicks and clacks caused by the mud-crabs who viewed our ship as a kind of cornucopia showering down such good things as empty tins which still well warranted the scouring of a cautious crabby claw. In between times we dug out jigger worms from our feet with long thin bodkins and poured vinegar into each other's ears to relieve heat pressure.

We were given during this period a very pretty example of the mischievous cunning which forms an all too common facet of the African mentality. My friend John Norris had flown by charter plane to Kilwa Masoko and having landed safely on a bush airstrip, had duly solved our engine trouble. When he departed two days later he promised to do his best to find for the ship a good marine engineer in Dar-es-Salaam. Sure enough, a few days later an African appeared out of the blue complete with a signed contract and a letter from Norris to introduce Chanda M..., an expert engineer recommended by one of the Port engineers in Dar-es-Salaam. He added that on signing the contract he had paid Chanda a substantial advance on his wages. To cut a long story short, we set out on a test run and it was thanks solely to instant action by the Nahoda and Ali that the dinghy was not crushed to matchwood between the *Gloria Scott,* proceeding out of control in reverse, and the side of the jetty. Out we shot and then stalled. Again the engine was started and proceeding in a series of fearsome jerks we covered two miles only to stop with a broken driving chain. There we remained tossing and wallowing for fourteen hours before we could effect a repair, and on regaining our moorings I gave myself the pleasure of violently expelling Engineer Chanda who vanished over the hill at a high rate of knots. By that curious grapevine telegraph of Africa, we came to know the truth within a few days. The real Chanda M..., after signing his contract and accepting his money, decided not to leave Dar-es-Salaam after all and had thereupon passed on the job to an out-of-work pal, having no engineering qualifications whatsoever, and supplied him with the necessary papers and permission to use his name. As one does not play jokes with the sea, I saw nothing funny in the situation and the matter was reported to the Police who, having admitted that the man had connived and executed a criminal offence, took out a warrant and, to judge by results, conveniently forgot about the matter.

The days had become swelteringly hot and the water correspondingly alluring. It used to be a standing joke between my brother and myself that when diving into the sea there was always the chance of meeting something unpleasant on its way up. This kind of jest has a way of coming home to roost. We had lost an anchor and an irreplacable length of rope in fairly deep water in the estuary and, after many hours of grappling along the bottom, we got into something heavy, almost certainly the lost anchor. Ghilani, despite his seventy years and as ever full of pluck, tore off his djellabeh and dived from the dinghy, down into the depths on the chance that he might reach the fifty-foot length of rope floating above the anchor ring. The rest of us, armed with rifles, kept a wary eye for shark. Ghilani reappeared after an astoundingly long period under water, — he was distinguished for the gill-like prowess of his lungs, — and was dragged into the dinghy. I was in a thoroughly dirty mood, warning one and all that it was a case of either recovering the anchor or rotting for eternity over the spot where it had been lost. After which I stripped, took a very deep breath and dived. A few yards below the surface I got a grip on the grappling line and fairly whizzed downwards in a headlong glide. The jade green grew rapidly darker and the thought had just crossed my mind that I must allow sufficient time for the return journey before my breath failed when, catching a faint glimpse of something immediately below, I plunged yet deeper on the chance that it might be a coil of the rope floating in mid-depth. The green was now very murky and, still swimming slowly downwards, I realised suddenly with an inexpressible thrill of horror that the object glimmering beneath me was something large and pale and fleshy. Kicking madly I shot for the surface at a speed that took me over the side and into the dinghy like a porpoise into a net. I cannot say for certain what it was that I saw in that horrible opaque depth, for the Kilwa estuary has none of the clarity of the open tropic sea, but I should guess that it was either a jewfish or a fairly large squid. Whatever it was, I had the utmost objection. We never recovered the anchor and had to purchase another from a passing dhow.

As a general rule, Ghilani and I took a very poor view of anybody swimming beyond the immediate vicinity of the ship's side owing to the likelihood of barracouda and to a lesser degree the odd shark.

But with the stubbornness of her sex Anna persisted in swimming where she pleased until one day when we were visited from the shore by Dmitri Loupis. After wandering in many strange corners of the globe, he was trading for a time in

Kilwa Masoko wherein he had rendered us invaluable assistance.

"I too lost an anchor from my schooner," he said, contemplating the smiling face below in the water. "It was in Port Sudan."

"Well?"

"A man on the spot volunteered to dive down and get it for a shilling."

"I hope you paid him."

"That was three years ago, and he is still down there with the anchor. We saw nothing," he added quietly, "just a little blood on the surface."

The tale was so salutary that I asked him if it were really true.

"On my honour," he replied, "and I can tell you something else that would strain the credulity of anyone who had not experienced the extraordinary ferocity of some types of shark. Off Kangaroo Island, near Australia, a White Death shark bit off the propellor of my schooner when we were proceeding at full speed and left a complete ring of serrated ivory teeth embedded in the wood around the propellor shaft. Nice neighbours! So have a care, dear lady, to do your swimming in the shallows."

The mouth of the estuary, edged by reefs stretching out like great arms into the Indian Ocean, lay some two miles distant from our anchorage and offered excellent opportunities for trolling by night providing that one kept a wary eye on the white line of foam marking those deadly coral barriers. Anna and I spent many evenings together in the outboard dinghy, trolling up and down in the swell of the ocean, that slow deep majestic swell spangled with the reflection of tropic stars above and the glow of tiny organisms swimming far below. I have never experienced a greater sense of loneliness and of my own complete insignificance than during those hours of darkness rolling and heaving on a fire-flecked sea beneath a fire-flecked sky. Normal things guised themselves in weird interpretations, so that the high-pitched shriek of the reel shocked the senses and the sudden strike of a fish with its swirl of phosphorescent flame became in a instant the grasp and glare of a monster.

Our nocturnal trolling yielded mixed bags of Barracouda, Kingfish and koli-koli but on one occasion Anna hooked into something of a very different character.

We were on the point of turning back into the mouth of the estuary and were over rather deep water when there came a tremendous screech from her reel and the heavy game rod commenced to bend and bend until the tip was only a matter of inches above the surface. Anna had clapped on the brakes as the great fish tore toward the coral reef and I could see from the tensity of her body that she was straining every muscle in her efforts to bring him round.

"It's too heavy," she gasped, "I can't even turn the reel handle."

"Shall I take it?"

"No... no... no! It must be a big shark or... here it comes!"

The line raced round the stern, as Anna and the rod thudded against the railings. I had no fear that the fish could break loose, for the line was 120 lb. test capable of holding a 1,000 pounder and fitted with twenty feet of wire cable leader. This comforting thought had scarcely passed through my mind when, with a sharp click, the metal guide at the rod tip was torn away. Anna pumped with all her strength as the fish dived deeper and, as a last desperate measure, clapped on her ratchet brake. For a moment the reel revolved with a long drawn-out scream and then ran silently. The teeth of the ratchet had been stripped as though made of china.

"I can't hold it, I can't... my God, it's gone!"

She reeled in and together we examined the line by the light of a flash lamp. The immensely strong wire leader had been sawn through immediately below the swivel, and we looked at each other blankly.

"What was it?" she asked, rubbing a bruised arm.

"Heaven knows," I said. "But whatever it may have been it was something extremely large. To judge by this broken trace and the damage to the rod and reel I doubt if any woman has ever fought and lost a bigger fish! You did magnificently and if it hadn't been for the breaking of the wire..."

I could have added that she would probably have landed a woman's World Record.

Defeated, tired, yet strangely well content, we started up the little outboard and set out on our return journey to the ship. A breath of wind carried the smell of the jungle, warm and cloying as decaying nectar. From the deep bush of Kilwa Kisiwani the call of a night bird echoed faintly across the water now dark no longer but paling under a phantom radiance as the edge of the tropic moon rising beyond the distant tree tops pierced their tangled crests into a lattice-work of white fire. It was good to be alive.

There are few things more attractive in the open air than the aroma of a wood-fire at dawn, and I sniffed appreciatively as I wandered along the shore in the early morning towards a faint blue haze of smoke arising from behind a clump of mangoes. Three natives were squatting at their ease around a fire of coconut husks while they devoured the carcass of a large Hawksbill turtle whose shell, glittering and gorgeously mottled, lay among the dead palm fronds like the shield of some fallen Trojan warrior. We chatted together in a horrible mix-

9

ture of Swahili and pidgeon English, in course of which the men informed me that they were the crew of a small dhow which had arrived last night after a long journey from Pemba Island, some way north of Zanzibar, down the Mafia and so to Kilwa. They must have been first class seamen to have come through at all in a boat which was little more than a split tree-trunk with a mast stepped in its middle. The meaning of courage is the most inexplicable thing in the world, and I have long ago given up even trying to understand it. These natives who would have run like the wind if I had raised my hand to them or at the very sight of Jum-Jum, thought nothing of risking their lives on a long sea journey in a craft so crazy that I would not have gone with them at any price.

Pemba Island is interesting on account of its sacred Cat-fish. Tucked away in the bush there is a small pool of fresh water which, though deep, is only some three feet across, resembling a natural well, and it is here that the officiating priest, for the price of an offering of eggs, squats in the early dusk and, stirring the water with a stick, commences to mutter and chant his ancient spells. And it always happens! The head of a large and revolting Cat-fish, all mouth and whiskers, suddenly rising up almost blocks the pool. The sacred creature is then fed, daintily taking the eggs one by one from the hands of the priest until, having disposed of the offering, it submerges slowly from sight beneath the muddy water.

CHAPTER 14

DESERT ISLAND

Two days prior to our escape — I can use no other word — from Kilwa Masoko we were joined by Curly Klein who had most sportingly volunteered to look after the engine and had come up from Lindi for that purpose. As things turned out, the presence of this calm, steady-eyed man with his expert knowledge of mechanics was little short of an act of God, for I hate to think what would have happened to us and the ship if we had been dependent upon an African fundi, a type of engineer just capable of dismantling a cigarette lighter providing that he is not expected to put it together again.

Official confirmation had come through from the International Game-Fish Association that our Dorado Dolphin was the new World Record, so we were feeling very bucked with life as we loaded the *Gloria Scott* with canisters of water and fuel in readiness for our departure on the morrow. By ten o'clock at night nothing remained to be done save endure the gasping, sweating hours until the dawn, hours enlivened by the most prolific display of lightning that I have ever beheld. A ripple of fire, at one moment blue, then red, then orange, depending on the local atmospheric conditions, waxed and waned along the whole circumference of the horizon. In an oppressive silence disturbed by neither wind nor thunder, shafts of fork lightening shot like silver veins across the glare of the sheet lightning scorching the sky beyond the jagged black crests of the African hills. It looked like the death of a world.

We were up anchor and away with the first light. It was

marvellously invigorating to be free of that turgid estuary and rolling once more in the clean blue slash of the sea with the breakers hissing and spurting along the coral reef which pointed our way to Songo Songo. Anna had the onus of watching our trolling lines from the stern while I kept a look-out for swordfish from the harpoon platform. We were rolling merrily along towards the palms of Songo Songo already gilded by the setting sun when there came a tremendous strike on Anna's rod, three hundred yards of line whizzing out despite all her strength plus the brakes; then, as the fish turned in a wide sweep the line went dead. On reeling in, we saw that the steel hook had been bitten through like a rotten carrot and savage tooth marks scarred the wooden lure.

I was trolling with light tackle and just as we were slowing for our night anchorage off the northern tip of Songo Songo my line came up with a jerk and then ran off in a long steady pull.

"Hell! I'm caught in the coral," I shouted. Although I pumped and braked, the reel continued to revolve and with only a few yards left on the spool the whole mechanism seized. By this time the anchor had gripped and Ali went off in the dinghy to free my line from the coral but — "It's a big fish, Bwana," he shouted exultantly peering down through the clear water—"Plenty food for supper." Sure enough my coral spire turned out to be an 80 lb. Cavalli Jack which had been quietly drowned without so much as a leap, and that night it furnished five hungry mortals, not to mention Jum-Jum, with an evening meal almost as good as swordfish steaks.

After supper we hung over the stern a powerful kerosene light which turned the immediate water into an oasis of clear shining jade through which there flashed and twinkled a myriad of tiny creatures. Slim garfish darted about on the surface, spearing their prey with their long jaws, while the hosts of fish fry swept across in torrents of shimmering silver. At the very edge of the light zone two pale shapes scouted stealthily up and down on the watch for stragglers; once they shot into full view, all eyes and tentacles, and out again behind a blur of black sepia as Anna poked at them with the gaff. Several varieties of beetle and a dragon-fly with a six-inch spread to its speckled wings hummed around the lamp despite the fact that we were anchored half a mile from the island, and these were joined by a Hummingbird Hawk moth distinguished by a most curious ivory white mark across the body behind the thorax exactly as though the creature had been saddled.

The lights were out and the ship had settled down for the night when there commenced a sharp pattering as though showers of pebbles were striking the deck and cabin top. Almost asleep, I was vaguely puzzling over this curious noise when something horny with unpleasantly barbed feet marched across my face. I flew upright so violently that I knocked my skull on the bulkhead. A horrid scurrying and rustling filled the cabin.

"Anna," I announced, "we are not alone."

I was about to add some jewel of witticism when I was effectively silenced by another outbreak of barbed feet scampering down my bare chest.

"There's something disgusting in my hair," cried Anna from the nether darkness of the cabin.

I scratched a match and the dim light of our candle dispelled the gloom. The walls and the roof, the backs of the books and even the rifles in their clips were streaked with racing shadows. From the galley beyond arose a sound of rustling paper as though a thousand eager fingers were exploring our reserves of flour and sugar.

We armed ourselves with a sandal apiece.

"You take one side and I'll take the other and we'll meet on the ceiling," said Anna, and the work began.

Now, to use the term cockroaches is to mislead the reader into visualising that homely little beetle that skulks in attics and dark corners of old kitchens. The little innocents! This flying horde of cockroaches from Songo Songo, descending upon us out of the night like an invasion of locusts, was composed of flat-bodied, armoured beetles of anything up to three inches in length with enormous antennae and sharp, thorny legs that carried them around the cabin and over our persons with a speed that turned one dizzy to behold.

Whack! Whack! Thwack! went the sandals, amid a revolting turmoil of crunching and squashing and plopping.

"I've killed twenty-six," Anna gasped.

"Hold still!" I cracked her across the back of the neck just in time to prevent a positive grandfather among beetles from vanishing down her nightie. "That brings me level," I announced with grim satisfaction.

At this point an outburst of yells and bangs arose from the crew's quarters and grew rapidly into a pandemonium. It was comforting to know that others were involved and with renewed energy we threw ourselves once more into the fray. An hour later the ship was clear save for splodges and smears and huge fragments of beetle all over the place and, snapping our fingers triumphantly at the woods of Songo Songo, we settled down to brew ourselves a huge pot of tea.

We headed due north on the following morning under ideal trolling conditions for the big fish. The whole glorious panorama of sea and sky merged into one limitless universe of hot blue glass without cloud or ripple, and eighty feet below our keel the coral patches flitted by like dark shadows on pale turquoise sand. Once, we were passed by three magnificent Leopard Rays flapping along in line ahead formation, the tips of their spotted wings curling up above the surface and their long black tails complete with triple daggers trailing out behind them. I would like to know why the majority of the Raiide of all types invariably travel with the same military precision. For some time after the passing of the Leopard Rays there was not a fish to be seen and this tended to confirm my theory that the big fellows had moved up to the northern portion of the Mafia channel in pursuit of the schools, a sure sign that we were nearing the dreaded period of the changing monsoon.

The dice was against us with a vengeance but I swore by all my Gods that somehow we should succeed in our objective of proving that both free life and great fish could be found in the virtually unexplored waters of the Mafia even if we had to face the hazards of the South-West monsoon beyond the outer reefs. I could visualize that line of smooth coral cliffs plunging sheer into 600 fathoms of water, the horizon stretching across the wastes to Australia, and my heart sank at the thought. I was curled up on the harpoon deck gloomily listing the risks which we should have to run thanks to our delay at Kilwa Masoko when, as though in red-hot sympathy, the engine gave vent to a fearsome noise and promptly stopped.

There we lay, rolling slowly on the slight swell which had come up after mid-day, and as completely helpless as a duck with one wing. Some two miles distant there arose a tiny island fringed with white sand and outcrops of rock rearing up through a maze of bush and palm trees like the remains of some ruined castle. Reach that island we must before the weather

changed. The Nahoda scanned the skyline anxiously and muttered in his beard as he watched the black fangs of coral
through which the sea ran in long eddies and swirls. The reefs
stretched away for a mile or more on two sides of us, and there
was no cause for rejoicing on the *Gloria Scott*. We tried in vain
to rig sails from the canvas deckhouse covers. There was only
one thing to do and situated as we were in those reef-strewn
waters and, as it turned out, with a Kaskazi coming up, it is no
exaggeration to state that it is thanks solely to our little Seagull
outboard motor that we escaped from a very unpleasant situation. I managed to clip it on the side and slowly... slowly...
it drove the 25-ton ship yard by yard to the comparative safety
of the island.

Down rattled the anchor and up went one vast sigh of relief
in English, Danish, Arabic and Swahili, and the puissant Klein
was shoulder deep in the engine before the flukes had gripped
the bottom of the sea. Somebody came to inspect us as promptly as any harbour official, for a high dorsal fin flickered wickedly above the surface, slowly circled the ship and passed from
sight.

"We're over coral, so we should get plenty of fish," Anna
remarked.

"Certainly, my dear girl," I agreed, "and why on earth
haven't you put out a line?"

She did. Instantly there came a shriek from the reel, a short,
sharp fight and she landed a beautiful 15 lb. Grunter, all amber and blue stripes.

"You had better leave the pan fishing to me," she observed,
"except when it is a matter of pulling in a dead fish!"

"Watch me, woman," I replied.

I cast out and spent the next sixty minutes with my hook
jammed in a ridge of coral, during which time inspiration spoke

through my lips and Jum-Jum hid himself in his old funk-hole.

Later Anna and I set out in the dinghy, gliding across a lagoon carpeted with mauve-coloured coral polyp which shimmered through the crystal water like a wonderful bed of violets. We beached the boat and pushed through the bush, only to come suddenly upon something which halted us in our tracks. I felt Anna's hand tighten on my arm.

From the sandy soil protruded an arrangement of coral slabs planted carefully on end to form an oblong. There was no doubt about it. It was a nameless human grave. Beyond in a small clearing of the bush lay traces of a camp, the fire-blackened earth littered with split coconuts, scraps of fish net and a broken spear shaft. Somehow there was an impression that the debris had been there for years.

It was hard work to cut our way through the mesh of thorny closely entwined vegetation but eventually we succeeded in reaching the point of the island. Personally I was by no means sorry to leave the bush, for every shrub and stunted tree seemed to be draped with a web supporting a large knobby-bodied spider with a four-inch spread of black and red legs which left a great deal to be desired, and sure enough, staring up lustfully at coconuts instead of watching my steps, I blundered into a horrible gelatinous mess which instantly enveloped my face and limbs and even my old briar pipe. I have no memory of actually bounding through two thorn bushes, though Anna swears that it was a spectacle marvellous to behold.

But it was heaven itself on the white coral sand beyond the palms where we threw off our brief garments and wandered naked under the lime trees, plucking fruit and jumping into the crystalline water just to have the thrill of climbing out again into the hot sun. It was all joy and glory, and fragrant in its primitive sweetness.

The greater part of the day passed in studying the varieties of marine creatures which had established themselves in the inner lagoon. Here were gardens of loveliness inhabited by death and agony. Above the shimmering violet grottoes there swam flamboyant shapes resembling bundles of scarlet feathers rather than fish, every plume-like fin equipped with a needle-point, a hollow core and a poison sac as venomous in result but far more agonizing than that of a cobra. But even worse than these Fire fish are their co-inhabitants, the Stone fish. The latter, perhaps the most shocking creation in all Nature, is a small insignificant creature a foot or so in length, a dirty grey in colour and, unless one has the fortune to discern a pair of brilliant topaz-yellow eyes, most difficult to perceive as it lies among the sea rubble. From its back bristle fifteen poisoned spines and, lacking a hospital within easy reach, a wound from those spines is enough to justify suicide if one possesses the means. It is no rare occurrence that men wounded in the foot by these fish have amputated the limb there and then with any handy knife rather than endure the agony of the poison eating through the veins. The victims are driven insane, striking and biting at all who approach them, and lucky is he who loses only a limb and not his life. While poking about among the coral, I became aware of two glittering golden eyes staring up at me and, though the fish was only a yard away, I had great difficulty in tracing the outline of its body against the dead grey boulders. I heaved a lump of coral on top of the thing but wriggling from under, it slipped away into the shadows of deeper water.

On every side lithe green Sea-scorpions darted about in disconcerting numbers, striking vigorously at the rod of my collecting net. We were wading along cautiously when we espied beneath the roots of a flowering pink coral something which from its size and vague outline we took to be a crayfish. But these were nervous waters and instead of grabbing it for the pot I took the precaution of first uprooting the pink coral, whereupon there appeared not a crayfish as we had fondly expected but a Sea-scorpion of a type which, so far as I am aware, is unknown to science. This horror was a full six inches in length, with a pale grey body two inches wide, and brilliant red legs. It cared not a damn, pursuing its way through slits and crevices while, with knees knocking with fear and a heart greedy to possess, I made abortive efforts to corner it until, after one tremendous strike at the net, the creature slid safely through a crack in a rock.

On the southern end of the island the variety of life both in the lagoon and along the outer reef justifies a certain amount of description and, I venture to think, would interest those who are not in the ordinary way drawn to the study of marine fauna. In the low Spring tide a large portion of the lagoon became for a few hours little more than a waste expanse of pools and sea-weed through which one wandered, now ankle-deep, now knee-deep. Amid the dark fronds of the weed glimmered the most fantastic starfish, some field-grey in colour, covered with points and spirals of brilliant scarlet while others were green spiked with orange or black spangled all over with tiny spots like a shimmering golden dust. These were all fingered-starfish but other varieties resembled octagonal pincushions. Fine shells, particularly the glistening Leopard Cowrie which polishes its own roof by means of a membrane, the spiked Scorpion shell and the Cassis Rufa, were plentiful amid the weed through which there occasionally protruded a thing like an upraised hand dipped in blood. This was the Red Finger Sponge and might have come straight from the haunted chamber in Sir Walter Scott's *Betrothed*.

The open pools were dappled with huge anemones, eighteen inches across, of a wonderful malachite green or grey edged with violet, each being the habitat of an identical community consisting of a small fish banded black and white with brilliant yellow fins, which lives there for the protection afforded by the folds of the anemone, and a coterie of tiny, rose-pink crabs which, when disturbed, take up battle stations, one behind the other, with claws extended defiantly in the direction from which danger threatens.

On rare occasions a lovely thing resembling a loose flower petal of delicate pink edged with purple or vermilion spotted with white undulated through the crystal water. This was a curious form of sea snail, shell-less and with telescopic feelers sticking up from its head and two circular, escalloped pads beneath, while the whole rear of the body, being covered with gelatinous protuberances and exactly resembling the coral polyp, were obviously for purposes of camouflage.

But there is a dark and more sinister side to this world of colour and fairy shapes, and beware the careless walker in the wastes of the low tide. Thousands of black sea-eggs, spined like a chevaux de frise, await the unwary foot and break off easily in the flesh, resulting in the most agonising pain. Through years of experience, one discovers that Nature has provided one undignified alleviation, namely, to urinate immediately on the afflicted locality and, believe me, the pain is such that if a little extra assistance is needed one suffers from no false modesty in hailing the passing stranger.

Everywhere lay the sea-slugs, sausage-shaped monstrosities of mottled brown, orange and red, which had the power of discharging a horrible viscid creamy substance resembling fine vermicelli. In one pool we came upon an infant Torpedo ray which, when touched, shot the arm to the shoulder like an electric bullet. This shock from a little creature of no more than eight inches gave one to think what would happen if one contacted its parents which have a discharge of 200 volts. Incidentally, these weird fish are believed to descend into the depths to recharge their electric power centres after use.

The whole sea-bed swarmed with things like huge worms spawned from a nightmare. These loathsome objects, varieties of *synapta maculata,* were coloured a pale, saffron brown mottled with black or more rarely a dappled pink, and presented a most unpleasant spectacle crawling and probing through the sea-fans and feeling their way along the coral ridges in search of prey. Their heads were a mass of clutching, febrile antennae like handfuls of tiny serpents that touched and explored every crevice in the rocks with a horrible eagerness. The specimen in the photograph was eight feet along when fully extended but, at the touch of a finger, turned instantly into a lump of immobile pink mucus.

In contrast was the Horned Trunk fish, a little animated creature contained in a boxlike case complete with horns and a projecting snout, and mottled all over with emerald and turquoise blue which darkened or lightened in sympathy with its surroundings. It was a charming friendly little person, and Anna spent some time in getting matey with one of them by the simple process of stroking it under the chin with a long stick. For a quarter of an hour it hung motionless in the water, with only its fins vibrating, and if a fish could purr then that fish certainly did. It followed Anna around the pool and they parted with mutual regret. In death, the Horned Trunk fish, and also its relative the Box-fish, possesses a most curious characteristic, for their bodies remain hard and brittle and if dangled from a post they will swing in the direction of any forthcoming storm or high wind several hours in advance of its advent and while still in conditions of tropic calm. I know an air station in Africa that employs the corpse of a twelve-inch Box-fish, hanging from the flag staff, for all wind warnings and finds the movements of this grotesquely shaped fish body to be extraordinarily accurate.

The outer reef exposed only at low tide was a creeping study in black and white. On that ribbon of blackish grey coral a hundred yards in width, every pool, crystal clear above its sandy bottom or strewn with bleached coral like a fossilized boneyard, was alive with the stealth of black sea-spines, black sea slugs and febrile black feather stars resembling a cross between a spider and an octopus. In one such pool we came upon a jet black *synapta* banded with white rings; while in another, above a grim carpet of feather stars, two caterpillar shapes covered with pink hairs hung motionless in the clear water. They were sea centipedes whose touch necessitates morphia. Sometimes the motif of black and white would be broken by the lovely floating patches of red and magenta sea snails with their protruding horns, while one strange variation of a mottled yellow-brown colour was equipped with a horned head and a second pair of horns on the neck, the creature ending in a circular, barrel-shaped base covered with gelatinous spines. Sea snakes, banded in black and white, combined with vicious Moray eels to keep one on the alert. I was attacked at lightning speed by one of the latter and bitten below the knee, but fortunately the big Morays kept to the deep water. Throughout the pools of the outer reef even the fish were en suite with the depressing colour scheme, the exception being a darting glorious fragment of sapphire that, occasionally flashing through the water, conveyed an enamelled luminosity.

A pile of sea rubbish had been washed amid the rocks and from beneath this jumble of bamboo and seaweed came a pair of arms, writhing and groping, to be quickly followed by a third. A shape, dimly seen in the shadowy heap, slithered suddenly into the daylight. It was a large octopus of the type aptly named Horridus, of a dirty ochre hue mottled and splotched with brown. I had no compunction in ending its evil days with my coral pick, for in very truth is this creature the lurking death to every other denizen of the deep that comes within the power of its tentacles. At the stroke of the pick a spasm of colour, one can only describe it as a flare of livid greenish black, flashed instantaneously over its body, the tentacles groped, curled, and then the whole vile organism sprawled among the seaweed. In attempting to describe the death spasm of the octopus one realizes yet again that there exist amid the coral reefs variations of colour that are nameless to man.

The sea-spines were an ever-present menace. The majority were ugly little bundles of black bayonets in miniature with here and there a lilac-hued variety. But on one occasion, however, we discovered the veritable emperor of sea-spines, a magnificent creature of more than a foot across and covered with six-inch salmon pink spikes banded with white. The top of the body was decorated with a five-pointed star of rich magenta checkered with luminous blue. After taking notes and measurements we left this rare creature, radiating with colour and dagger points, to the quiet sovereignty of its pool.

As one works the reefs and contemplates the marvellous Intelligence that looms behind the design of each strange, exquisite or terrible form of life, one sees the atheist in his true light. Here is the living force of God operating through the veins of Nature. A peace beyond understanding steals through one's being and imperceptibly the mind becomes focused to the utmost of its capabilities upon the marvellous pageantry that, living, breeding and dying, reflects the perfection of the Supreme Artist.

CHAPTER 15

DANCING MOON

My reference to the place as Spider Island evidently tickled Ali's fancy, for on the morrow I found the words printed on the shore in huge letters, for which purpose the rascal had slipped across in the dawn.

We were stranded for two days and two nights in the outer lagoon while Klein strove to fit a new big-end under conditions which proved both his tenacity and his skill. There was space for only one body in the engine-room, so we were free to dispose of our attention elsewhere which, off a lonely atoll, meant simply the marine life. And what a world of dreams it was.

We were in comparatively deep water and the vista below bore not the faintest resemblance to that of the reefs and shallows described in the previous chapter. The outer lagoon, though thirty feet deep beneath our keel, was of such marvellous clarity that not only the shape of the ship but even our own shadows as we craned over the rail were clearly shown on the bottom of the sea. White patches of sand separated the ridges and hillocks of coral shining beneath us into a series of tropical rock gardens in which Nature, with her peerless taste, had left the more brilliant colours to the fish and relied on the artifice of shape and pastel shades for the great panorama of the marine world itself. Above a profusion of pale yellows, browns and mauves, which were the flowering mantles of the Organ-pipe and Brain corals, there arose delicate chalices of coppery green intermixed with spires of rose pink shading down to the rich glow of amber. Grey sea-ferns and lace corals, jutting forth like

the gargoyles of a Gothic church, emphasized in their very som-
breness the fragile waving beauty of the seascape stretching
away through grottoes and pinnacles and ridges to lose itself
in dim green-lit distances. It was a world flashing with life.
Schools of Tanda-tanda, a small fish of brilland yellow striped with blue, swimming in and out of the spires mingled
with another species of vivid sapphire shading into green and
deep purple, and yet for all their loveliness, paling into insignificance whenever they were joined in their carefree flight
by the Rainbow fish in his livery of emerald green slashed and
veined with pale pink, scarlet and luminous mauve. At the
lower depth there moved the more sedate denizens, striped
Grunters and blood-red rock cod with their heavy jowls and
spikes, searching for crabs amid the coral polyp in company
with a lovely fish whose amber-coloured head glowed in startling contrast to the uniform ivory tint of its body, fins and tail.
Long-snouted Coral fish swimming slowly through the marine
grottoes appeared as black velvet discs until, suddenly touched
by the rays of the sun through the water, as by magic they
were transformed into plates of gold.

Once, a rare Unicorn fish, black with a white fan-shaped
tail, drove through the pageant, its little lance sticking out
before it like some doughty champion hurrying to the Lists,
and the advent of a school of Kingfish sent a bejewelled wave
of colour across the sea-bed as the smaller denizens rushed for
the shelter of nooks and crannies amid the coral. From the bar-
renness of a tiny ship and a desert island, we looked down into
the gorgeous courts of the Medici.

I caught a Tanda-tanda for our specimen collection only to
receive yet another lesson in that almost incredible swiftness
which in the tropics forms the worst characteristic of Nature's
attack. The fish bounding from the deck struck me on the

hand, inflicting a small but deep wound. The spines of all coral fish are poisonous in a greater or lesser degree and I spent the next five minutes sucking the wound and spitting out the blood before finally soaking my hand in alcohol. The prompt treatment did the trick and there were no ill effects except inflammation. I was rapidly coming to the conclusion that my sole purpose in life was to be the toy of insects and small creatures with spikes.

But despite the marine beauties we were far from comfortable in our position, for both the weather and the sea were highly treacherous at this period of the changing monsoon and, though the Nahoda insisted on keeping watch over the anchor chain for forty-eight hours at a stretch, even so we had to alter position more than once owing to drag. On the third morning the vicinity of the ship was disturbed by rising dorsals and the dry rasping blowing noise of a school of Blackfish or small whale which passed within a few yards of us. The Kaskazi was threatening again and the whole of the eastern horizon had become dark with thunder clouds whose high-nosed crests bore an almost ludicrous resemblance to a line of House of Hanover portraits in profile.

Klein had finished his repairs and after a general conference it was decided to chance it and press on in the direction of Okusa, a desolate uninhabited island.

For hours we rolled and pitched our way through an endless vista of angry wave tops, a vista broken at last by a tiny knob of green trees rising abruptly above a maelstrom of leaping bursting spray. It was impossible in such a sea to attempt a landing on Okusa and so there was nothing to be done but lie for the night off the tip of the reef.

It was a night of great Voices, primeval yet strangely exhilarating, when the puniness of man swings and bobs and rolls and spins in the blast of elemental Eternity. Time had died and our whole world existed only in the thunder of black water and the pale whistling slash of spume hurtling downwind like tatters from torn shrouds. Beyond the fury of the breakers the trees of desolate Okusa seemed to strain their very roots to the same maddened dance that sent the stars a'whirling and a'reeling above our mast-tip. It was only with the glimmer of dawn that we eventually regained some sense of reality.

The difficulties of the night were not improved by the fact that shortly before dawn we had to move anchorage to another point beyond the reef owing to that bane of our existence, the unreliability of the Admiralty charts. The depths in fathoms as shown on these blue-prints of the ocean bed were based on the Royal Navy Surveys of 1874 and 1875 and in some cases harked back to the French Survey of 1823. The information contained in the charts, despite a few modern alterations, was often dangerously misleading and on more than one occasion, when anchored off reefs and islands in what, according to the charts, should have been three fathoms or more of water at low tide, we had to move ship, sometimes in the dead of night, to avoid grounding; the eighteen feet of low ebb being in fact little more than five feet. The whole area from Kwale Island in the north, right down the Mafia Channel and the Kilwa Main Pass to Songa Manara in the south should be resurveyed.

The little hum-drum things presented in many ways the greatest strain of all to a woman. For instance, cooking. It was often so rough at sea that Anna had literally to tie up her saucepans with strings made of coconut fibre while she kept the Primus legs wedged in holes which she had drilled through the table top. Yet she always made out somehow amid crashing pots and wild flares of paraffin.

The final stage of our journey to Mafia covered ten hours

but the wind was dropping steadily and by the time that we caught a first glimpse of our destination faintly visible against the red-gold blaze of the dying sun, the calm of evening lay on the sea.

Mafia is a heavily wooded island and, as we stole in towards the shore, the atmosphere was so clear and pellucid that it seemed as though we were floating over the shadows of the great Gum Copal trees that towered above the narrow beach. For sheer beauty alone Mafia, its cool green woods poised between a limitless expanse of sea and sky, could hold its own with any island in the world. On the western side lay the great Channel strewn with reefs and mysterious little islands and protected all the year round from the worst of the monsoons. On the eastern side, which is the outer edge of the great submarine plateau known as the Mafia Shelf, the waters remained quite unexplored and, highly dangerous and fringed by an unbroken line of coral cliffs, were believed to be the hunting ground of monster fish. Mafia is thirty miles long and shaped like a pre-historic axe blade, its only industry being the export of copra, the dried coconut kernels from its palm forests, which afford a livelihood to the four or five white men composing the European population.

Here at last in this neglected island we were to receive encouragement and practical assistance. Jock Scott, the Resident Commissioner in Mafia, is himself not only a skilful fisherman but one of those rare men 'born to the job'. If the type of Jock Scott could be found more often among the District Commissioners of East Africa, the natives would have kept their reverence, and incidentally their liking, for the white man. His is the generosity of the sportsman combined with the integrity of the Crown, and there is nothing finer. The copra planters, De La Fontaine, Morgan and the Stanley brothers were all ex-naval men, good fellows and red-hot fishermen, and a more sporting set of men on a more lovely island it would be difficult to imagine. I was extremely interested to learn that De La Fontaine, when on patrol with his naval vessel in 1944 and having occasion to pass along the outer reefs of Songa Manara, had been forced to alter course to avoid the biggest Tiger shark which he had ever seen or dreamed of. He estimated that it was at least thirty feet in length and, bearing in mind that a shark will stay for many years in the same haunt, I agree with him that it was almost certainly the same monster which had passed us in the night.

After a week in the Rest House where we actually slept in beds and ate tinned food off a steady table—fantastic luxuries — we were off again, skirting the south end of the island to the Eastern Shelf where, in Chole Bay, we established our base amid the deserted ruins of what had once been the German centre of government. Chole was almost landlocked on three sides. The fourth opened into the great unexplored fishing waters stretching across thousands of miles from the Kinasi reef to the coast of Australia. A few yards out from the coral cliffs the sea bottom fell nearly two thousand feet sheer, and within a very short time the swell of the new monsoon battering against the ramparts would turn the whole coastline into a death-trap. We had not a moment to lose.

On our last night before departing for Chole Island I was awakened by the rhythm of the drums. The shadows of the palms beyond the verandah lay like a black tracery under the full flood of the moon and every frond drooped in the liquid silver sleep that belongs only to the tropic night. There is a primitive element anchored in the basic strata of one's being which quivers into life under a combination of certain sounds and scents, and I was vaguely conscious of a feeling of excitement, of animal anticipation, as I tried in vain to close my ears to the clear trilling of the cicadas and that slow passionate sensuous throbbing from the depth of the moon-drenched rain forest. A wave of perfume from a night flowering tree mingled with the bitter-sweet tang of a distant wood-fire. It was too much. I leapt from my bed and ran into the forest in search of the drums.

The path led through glades of silver and along dim avenues paved in a mosaic of light and shadow roofed over with branches where high overhead the bush-babies chattered and swung in silhouette against the stars. And ever the drums call-ed. I found myself at length in a clearing ringed with great trees and at the far end a long low hut of palm fronds under whose overhanging roof there squatted a line of women. A thin pencil of smoke scenting the air with its aromatic fragrance arose from the ashes of a wood-fire around which were group-ed the drums, painted and gleaming in the moonlight. A group of men half hidden in the shadows of the Gum Copal trees stood or crouched on the other side of the clearing. The throbbing rhythm lifted to a pitch that quickened the blood only to pause and subside into a muttering as a solo baritone voice as wild and virile as the trees that overshadowed the unseen singer, soared upwards in all the magnificent barbarism of a tribal song. The voice died away and as a last note melted in the si-lence the women on the opposite side of the glade broke into a high shrill cry sad and lingering as the wailing of lost angels. The baritone commenced the second stave. Again and again the performance was repeated until one's senses were drowsy with moonlight and the liquid beauty of that wonderful voice soaring triumphantly above the symbolic lament of Woman. As the song drew towards its close the two groups swayed out from the shadows into the full light of the moon and met and danced and whirled to the wild hot beating of the drums. Coconut husks filled with tembo, a white heady syrup distilled from the palms, were circulating freely and, little by little, the drums throbbed faster than ever, if somewhat irregularly, while the rhythm and animal cries of the dancers mingling with the voices of those who preferred to sing turned the scene into a medley of incipient lust. Some of the women had thrown off their upper garments, their splendid breasts shining like ebony in the moonlight while here and there a lighter-skinned girl flaunted the nudity of her pale bronze bosom before the grinning savage faces and the hands which clutched and touched and caressed in the whirling of the dance. Occasionally a woman would break loose from the revel to wander away almost casually, feigning unconsciousness that the man at her heels had cast off his simple cloth skirt and now pursued her vibrantly naked into the dim shadow-world of the great trees. It seemed to me altogether right that these men and women whose whole reaction to life was based simply on physical instinct should flee into the forest, into the very womb of Africa, for the primitive joy of their love-making.

Making my way homeward in the witching hour, the sounds of the drums and the cries and laughter grew fainter and fainter until there was nothing but the throbbing, that ageless hypnotic throbbing that plays on human hearts and human passions, to rival the night voices of the cicadas singing to the waxen moon above the palm trees.

CHAPTER 16

THE PASS OF SHARKS

Ali Mahommet Ghilani, our Nahoda, had returned to Zanzibar to see his sons, dhow captains from Muscat, and we had to take on another in his place, which brought unpleasant consequences. The sea journey from Mafia to Chole Island, though a matter of only twenty miles, is somewhat hazardous save at full tide and in daylight, for the charts which were made in 1875 are quite inaccurate owing to the growth of the sea bottom since that time, and the Channel itself running over great beds of coral is traversed at its narrowest point by a double line of grim niggerhead coral spires which may be passed only on the flood. We were late in leaving Mafia owing to one of those maddening combinations of circumstances which always arise when one is urgent to be away, and darkness had already fallen by the time that we entered the channel. We craned over the side and, watching by torchlight the great coral heads flitting under our keel, raised a warning shout to the Nahoda whenever a particularly loftylooking mass loomed in the water ahead. Four hours of this, and we were all heartily glad when the anchor rattled down off the great black shadow that was Chole Island.

Shortly before dawn, as ill-fortune would have it, a Kaskazi began to blow while the sea rose rapidly and rain, driven almost horizontally by the force of the wind, penetrated even into the cabin through every joint in the woodwork. A few minutes later a heavy shock beneath the hull caused the ship to tremble from stem to stern. Again and again an ominous grinding punctuated by a loud thudding noise vibrated through her timbers while with the rain lashing our bodies we strove to pull forward on the anchor chain. Six feet we gained and not an inch more, for the flukes after dragging from the sand patch in which we had been anchored had jammed in the coral bed which was now beating the life out of the ship. It was entirely the Nahoda's fault for not attending to the drag of the chain and with the brave little ship in jeopardy I think that he escaped over-easily with my punch which sent him into the scuppers. Klein had started the engine but we were jammed too firmly on the cursed coral and there was nothing to be done but wait for the last of the tide to drop. Then, when we hurried to inspect the damage, our hearts fell.

The steel false keel had been ripped loose from its rivets and now gaped beneath the woodwork, the copper plates covering the keel proper were badly buckled and a series of tears and jagged marks scarred the planking of the hull.

Was this the end? After all our efforts and a myriad unwritten difficulties overcome, were our hopes to finish thus? I was overwhelmed with such a wave of bitterness that I waded ashore by myself and sitting on a fallen palm tried to think things over. And the more I thought, the more I kicked against the pricks. It was almost as though an ill fate had interfered with our plans from the first. It had been our original intention in November to head for Mafia and its adjacent islands and waters but interested advice had sent us to Kilwa Masoko where we found that every bit of information which we had been given was strictly untrue; next, when we were on the very eve of heading, at long last, to Mafia, engine trouble had intervened and laid us by the heels for seven whole weeks; the engine finally settled, the engineer himself had departed; then, in the ensuing three weeks we had been betrayed firstly by the fake 'engineer' now sought by the Police, and then by an engineer who knew everything except engineering and who was so racked with T. B. that the mark of death was already upon him; finally, Klein had come forward and it had seemed that at last things might go ahead; but no sooner had we reached Mafia than our indispensable Nahoda had to leave, and this when the bad monsoon was about to set in, following the two perfect months which had wasted away while we lay helpless in Kilwa of vile memory. And now, having reached our *real* objective — the great unknown waters of the Kinasi Pass beyond Chole — there lay our little ship on the coral reef!

I was past cursing or weeping and plunked myself down on the mental rock that, whatever misfortunes had befallen us, after all these were in themselves a part of Adventure. Action, not brooding, must be the word.

The Nahoda was kicked ashore to raise every native in Chole who was capable of driving a nail through wood. The Jumbi or local headman buzzed about like an important bluebottle and assisted us in bringing ashore our principal gear and stores in case the ship sank in the rising tide. But the worst was avoided and, to cut short an altogether agonizing incident, repairs were effected within thirty-six hours which, though rough and ready in the extreme, should be sufficient, we hoped, to enable us to carry on. Glory be, and even the Nahoda was forgiven!

Now that the ship was safe, we were able to give attention to our island base, which can only be described as an infringement on Heaven's patent. It was a smallish island lusciously green and girdled with water of crystal clarity, and at the very point where the white sand met the shade of the palm trees a little coral-walled hut complete with palm-leaf roof offered a shelter from the elements. A large proportion of the jungle was composed of fruit-bearing trees which supplied our modest table with coconuts, oranges, grapefruit, mangoes and stafeli, while a very old Arab well encircled with two curious rings of stonework provided our drinking water. The natives themselves, occupying a straggling village tucked away in the vivid heart of the forest, were a dying race consisting almost entirely of ancient men and women who still preserved the natural courtesy which belongs to the Africa of the past. Word had got about that we were there in pursuit of the dreaded Pa Pa whose flesh would mean fat bellies for all, so we were duly made aware that both we and our purpose were welcome in their midst.

An old packing case was lugged ashore as Anna's dressing table. Very sensibly she had never faltered in her use of cosmetics throughout the expedition, merely altering the methods to fit in with the prevailing conditions. Face powder was impracticable owing to the wet heat, but face cream by day and skin food at night formed a simple but effective barrier against the greatest menace to a woman's peace of mind, the feeling that she is losing the feminine in the exigencies of a life that is basically masculine.

Though brilliantly skilful in her fishing and generally more practical than me even in such things as stripping a carburettor, she had a woman's wisdom to concentrate her best efforts in arranging tropical blossoms, collecting varieties of shells and cooking strange but very edible dishes from mixtures of bully beef, rice, fish and fruit. She was a perfect nuisance whenever she lost a fish on the line, but I never heard her complain in the face of domestic discomforts like brushing our teeth in salt water or the fact that our soles were adrift from our shoes.

At first it seemed to us that we lived sumptuously and for virtually nothing on this forgotten little coral island. One had but to pluck fruit from the trees, succulent oysters flourished at our very doorstep, and chickens and eggs were bartered for fish hooks. Even our camp table was adorned with lovely seashells which we used as vases for flowers which might have come from the garden of a Mandarin.

But despite all these pleasant conditions there was a characteristic of Chole Island which was eerie in the extreme. For a long time prior to 1914, the island had been the seat of the German Government for the whole of the Mafia area and, with admirable Teuton thoroughness, the Germans had erected for their Boma or government quarters not the clay walls and tin roof of a British Boma but a magnificent mansion with walls almost five feet thick, spacious windows and timbers for joists, window frames and door lintels of such admirable quality that they had withstood the vicissitudes of forty years of roofless ruination amid the heat and terrific rains of the tropics.

The German officials, residents and traders had built beyond this Boma a fine stone town of pleasant houses and shops interspersed with some very ancient Arab buildings and an Indian mosque.

Now, all was desert and ruin. The huge gaunt-faced Boma still reared its massive façade above the coral beach but the roof was gone and with it the great balcony, and what had once been windows and doors were now but gaping orifices overlooking the remains of the drill-yard and the state entrances beyond which lay the shore littered with shards of broken German pottery mixed with far older pieces of Chinese blue and white porcelain, much used by the Shirazi Persians who had a stronghold in the twelfth century on the neighbouring island of Juani. The street of private houses and shops had become a ghost town throttled in the death-grip of lianas and completely overgrown by the trees which threw a sickly green twilight over fangs of masonry that were once the home of men. A line of exquisitely blossomed Mtiwashetani or Devil trees, beneath whose perfumed branches Satan himself, sensible fellow, is believed to sleep, had survived the utter wreckage and, raising their orange-throated flowers to the sunlight, still enwrapped in their fragrance the ruins of the Double Eagle. In many ways our island was a 17th century-1914 edition of Songa Manara on a small scale and incidentally not a native would approach the vicinity of our camp after dark... For did we not dwell beside the place which was silent only by day?

Throughout these tiny, forgotten islands of the Indian Ocean the natives are remnants of expiring tribes containing few young people and a high proportion of congenital idiocy through inter-breeding. The pale bronze high-featured Shirazi Persian type is occasionally to be found among the prevailing negroid, and it is interesting to note that even to this day descent from the Islamic overlord carries with it a conscious superiority. Superstition is the bane of the people and the Devils of land, sea, ruin and forest occupy a very real place in their mental life. I do not believe that the white man will ever discover the fearsome clue leading back and back through time to that dark morass of the spirit in which are rooted beliefs common to almost every primitive race throughout the world. A clear example is to be found in the destruction of huts after death, a practice shared by such widely divergent races as Central American Indians, certain tribes of Africans and the Eskimos of the Arctic Circle. Fear is not only the common denominator; it is the fungus of the Ages.

The fishermen had a lot to say on the subject of the great fish which haunted the adjacent waters and especially the Kinasi Pass, the awesome gap leading from Chole bay into the Indian Ocean, and it transpired further that quite recently they had lost two or three of their small community, the poor devils being bitten in two by a shark when bathing up to their waists in the vicinity of our hut. It is only the tragic circumstances which prevent me from writing — this was most encouraging!

We lost no time in making an exploratory run through the Kinasi Pass, and a more grim-looking place I have seldom seen. At some early period the coral cliffs must have continued right across the bay from Miwi Island on the left to Chole Island on the right but the pounding of the Indian Ocean had broken down the bastion and now all that remained were a series of great blocks and turrets of coral rising twenty feet above the surface of the sea which tore between their bristling flanks at a tide rate of eight knots. Beyond this line the water became a marvellously clear deep blue through which one could discern not only the corals and sea-fans but even the colours of the fish — and very large fish they were — moving over the sea bottom sixty feet below; then the depth fell away in a precipitous drop and the water, now almost black, was tormented by such rips and eddies that we could make but feeble progress despite the full power of the engine. It was the finishing touch that this waste of darkened sea swirling between towers of coral resembling thunderheads solidified into stone should be the pass of sharks, the lurking place of the great man-eaters.

One morning we had just returned from trolling for Barra-couda when we were met by the Jumbi, an old but powerfully built native clad in a scanty cloth skirt and carrying a 16th century bowl and two Kaiser Wilhelm German beer mugs for our inspection.

"The Kinasi should be good for big fish," I said to him. "Have you lost any men there through overturned canoes and shark?"

"No, Bwana." He thrust out a scrawny arm, "Do you see that blue strip in the channel?"

"You mean just beyond the pale green water over the sand patch?"

"Yes. Well, that's where we've lost men in recent times. That blue strip is the swim of a killer shark from the point of the island there, through the narrow channel and so to the Kinasi, and then back again."

"Nonsense."

"It is the truth, Bwana," he said simply.

Something in the old man's manner impressed me.

"But what kind of shark? In the Kinasi, yes, but not in here..."

"Maybe it's an Amrani (tiger shark), maybe it's a Pingozi (hammerhead), I cannot tell, but I have seen his fins, that devil of cunning and wickedness, and I have seen his work. One man he bit in two, and he died; another he bit off his legs, and he died; and a third he bit off his arm, and he lived. You must get this shark, Bwana."

"I'll do my best," I assured the old man, conscious of a thrill of excitement as I watched that innocuous streak of blue running across the eau-de-nil of the shallows.

During the night our worst fears were realized. A rising wind accompanied by thunder and torrential rain announced the first stages of the breaking of the monsoon and within an hour the booming of the surf on the Kinasi reef, though three miles distant, had risen to a pitch that exactly resembled the traffic roar of a great city. These conditions continued for some days before settling into a period of intermittent storms and calms which caused us to keep a nervous eye on the south-east skyline whenever we were out from our anchorage under the lee of the island.

It had not taken us long to discover the virtues of Chole and now we were learning the disadvantages. The natives were indescribably lazy and this meant a continuous shortage of bait, for which we were largely dependent upon their fish traps. It boiled down simply to this. They preferred to risk their lives in the swim of a known killer rather than have the bother of laying nets for the bait which might rid their neighbourhood of this ever-present menace, and I confess that I contemplated the thought of their Jumbi being taken by a shark with the greatest equanimity. We had gone through too much, however, to be short-circuited by the indolence of the Chole Islanders and so, where money failed, violence worked and it was not long before a net organization was established though with poor results owing to the unsettled state of the sea.

There was another drawback to Chole of a much more malevolent nature, for the local shallows were alive with Sea-scorpions, strange dark green creatures not unlike a legless prawn adorned on the head with tufts of orange-coloured feelers. In contrast to their land namesake, these Sea-scorpions double up and strike *beneath* their bodies, the jab being so powerful that when touching one of them with a metal rod through six inches of water I could hear distinctly the 'ping' of the strike thrice repeated against the iron shaft.

It is dangerous to relax even for a moment in the backwaters of the tropics. Beneath the veneer of colour and beauty, many divers forms of destruction or injury strike through the fabric of life whenever opportunity offers or a momentary careless-ness creates the form of opportunity. The following is an excel-lent case in point. We were about to go trolling for Barracouda and in order to strap my revolver holster to my belt (in these sharky waters I never moved without my gun) I dropped my fishing gloves for a moment on the floor of our hut and then, picking them up again, ran down to the beach and into the dinghy. It was a perfect morning and, on reaching the *Gloria Scott,* we started the engine and headed out towards the coral spires of the Kinasi Pass, showing like a line of tiny blackened fangs against the blue haze of the Indian Ocean. I had strapped on heavy game harness and, settling the rod firmly in the butt socket around my waist, nothing remained to be done save tug at my right hand fishing glove which seemed to have lost its comfortable fit. Tug as I would, however, there remained a certain tightness across the back of my hand and a distinct lump as though a large oval cigarette was wedged between my skin and the glove. I was about to remove it casually when some queer prescience of danger flashed through my senses and, tearing off the glove, I looked. At first I was rooted to the spot, literally paralysed with horror and disgust while a cold sweat burst out on my forehead. Straight down the back of my hand from wrist to knuckles there stretched a villainous centipede. It was ginger in colour, very flat and broad, its many claws poised lightly against my flesh. After which there was a kind of hiatus in which I dimly remember wringing my hand and leaping clean over the top of the fishing chair simultaneously with the crack of the loathsome insect hitting the deck. I flattened it into a small omelette and felt like vomiting. It was a narrow escape from much pain and dolour.

Rather diffidently I was pulling on my gloves again when Anna hailed me from the harpoon platform.

"Do come and look at these jelly-fish," she cried, "they're simply marvellous."

I felt that I could do with something marvellous and hastened for'ard. At first sight, I could see precious little but as my eyes accustomed themselves to the play of blue light streaming down into the water, I forgot all about the erstwhile centipede in the wonderful spectacle which was unfolding beneath us. The depth of the sea was a close-packed mass of transparent mauve-tinted domes, floating, drifting shapes of such ghostly delicacy that even at a depth of fifty feet and more the submerged rays of sunlight suffused the lowest ranks in a soft violet glow and tipped in silver their trailing waving fringes. It was a bird's-eye view of the parachute invasion on the beaches of Normandy. For five wonderful minutes they streamed below us, a hazy avalanche of fairy umbrellas, all tilted at the same angle and impelling themselves forward by a pulsing of their domes so that the whole great host moved shuddering upon their way. Staring down at them, we lost all sense of depth and it seemed for the moment as though we and the ship were supported no longer by the water but embedded in a solid mass of violet-coloured jelly. A minute later, and the sun's rays streamed down into a blue emptiness. There was not a jelly-fish to be seen.

We had good sport on the fringe of the coral spires with Barracouda and Karembesi, and it was not until a ragged line of storm clouds boiled across the sun that we headed for home.

Night after night the formidable rains of the tropics swept across our island, roaring in a deluge outside the doorless entrance to the shack and soaking through the palm-leaf roof until we would be awoken by a dozen jets of water spraying upon our bodies or turning our camp beds into gutters. The uproar was as deafening as a Niagara of dried peas pouring through a sieve and wherever we dragged our beds, stumbling and blundering about in the darkness, we would be rediscovered by some cursed driblet whereupon this highly malignant form of musical chairs would begin all over again. Eventually we learnt to accept the inevitable and lie still providing that the water did not actually play on our faces. Our various attempts to repair the broken fronds in the roof were somewhat handicapped by the presence of mud nests of the size and texture of flower-pots occupied by a ferocious hairy-legged red fly with the stab of a miniature assassin. These things left us well alone so long as we returned the compliment but they let it be known that they considered our repairs to the roof as an unwarranted trespass.

Once we were almost blacked-out by a swarm of wild bees which invaded the hut in search of our remaining stock of sugar. I have always admired the courage of those experts who go about with a kind of visor of bees crawling all over their faces but to us it was sufficiently nerve-racking merely to drag out the sacks with the tips of our big-game rods. The only person who could afford to relax completely was Jum-Jum who snored his way through days and nights, waking only to consume hunks of Barracouda or chase through the forest after the Jumbi who, with cries of "It's not a dog! It's not a lion! It's a Shaitan!" showed a turn of speed remarkable in one of his years.

Nevertheless, despite bad weather and native trouble, life jogged along with a queer sense of expectancy amid the ruins and Devil Flowers of Chole.

CHAPTER 17

KINASI KILLER

A few nights later the wind had dropped and having run out a shark line baited with a 10 lb. Grunter and tied the end to a tree, I lay naked on the sweet coolness of the sand and watched the wonder of the tropic stars blazing above the black graceful forms of the palm trees outlined against the glow of the rising but still invisible moon. A glimmer of candlelight from the window of our hut made a tiny orange patch far away along the darkness of the shore. It was a night for dreaming; a night when memories, sweet and cherished fragments, came a'riding on the perfume of the nocturnal flowers to make one's heart pay ransom, and in such a place and on such an hour staring up at the serenity of heaven from a bed of snow-white sand, even my native skirt would have been an anachronism.

Midnight was already passed when lazily I tested the sharkline. It was taut. I pulled and quite slowly the slack was pulled out again.

"The line is caught around coral," I said to myself, giving it a mighty jerk. For a moment a loose coil lay on the sand, then inch by inch the line crept out until it stretched as taut as a harp string from the black waters to the black palm tree. I sat and waited.

Three hours crept past. Almost imperceptibly the tips of the palm fronds changed from drooping funeral plumes stained in midnight blue into sprays of diamond feathers poised and shimmering between the cold clear rapture of the stars and an over-shadowed earth. The moon, already declining from her zenith, flooded the whole expanse of the shore in a blaze of white fire against which, with an abruption almost agonizing to behold, lay the water's edge like the folds of a black velvet pall, solid, motionless, impenetrable. The purring of burrowing crabs rose and fell as though the very sand sighed in uneasy dreams. And yet despite the serenity of a world sleeping in moonlight, I was vividly aware of a feeling of evil founded perhaps on nothing more definite than the contrast on one hand between sheer beauty spiced with the hot voluptuous scent of the Devil flowers, burning like tiny orange flames amid the blue shadows of the palm trees, and on the other the curiously menacing immobility of the rope stretching across the sand like a taut thread of silver above a taut thread of black. But taut with what? Somewhere in those dark waters lay the answer.

The coral beds were exposed by now for a hundred yards' distance from the shore and following the line I splashed my way through the loneliness and desolation, leaping into the air every time that the vicious head and coils of a Moray eel spattered towards me across that wilderness of shining silver pools.

Still clutching the rope, I was thigh-deep in the shallows when the water in front of me was literally torn apart and a column of spray, glittering in the moonlight, shot high into the air. A great tail reared up and smote the surface like a mallet, sending wavelet after wavelet hissing across the glimmering coral ridges. There was an almighty jerk on the line and the next instant my feet had shot from under me and I went head over heels into the water. I came up gasping. There was not the slightest use in hunting around for the rope which had been pulled under the surface and in any case the end was firmly knotted to the palm tree. A wicked black dorsal fin tore across the silver path of moonlight, dipped in a long curl of foam and then tore back again. I had a fleeting glimpse of a rounded blunt-nosed head, curiously pale against the water, and a grinning mouth like a great dark gash that snapped and gaped and snapped again. Then the surface was once more still and nothing but a dim shiver of phosphorescence told of the fearsome thing lurking below.

On my journey back to the hut I think that the Moray eels must have leapt from me. The pools flew. Then once more I hurried back to the sea, armed with Anna in a Paris dressing gown, a rifle and a torch. The dorsal fin was cruising up and down again but with even more savage vigour, as though the shark sensed instinctively the fall of the tide.

"For God's sake don't put even your foot into the water," Anna whispered, her eyes following with a horrified fascination the silence and swiftness of the black triangle.

"Not I!" I assured her. "But keep the torch down. The moonlight is sufficient for me, if only the head breaks water."

Patiently I awaited my opportunity and then a pale mass rose abruptly to the surface some twenty yards distant. One glance was enough and I sent a bullet crashing through the evil head of the thing. I expected a turmoil to follow but instead the shark sank quietly beneath the surface and it later transpired that my bullet had cut the spinal cord at the base of the skull.

Ali had joined us by this time and together we hauled the ponderous weight towards the shallows. The tide was beginning to turn and I had to stay there for the remainder of the night to heave on the rope whenever the rising water offered a new opportunity to drag the shark nearer to the shore. I dared not leave it in deep water, owing to the ravages of Barracouda.

Dawn was streaking the sky when at last amid the cold, dreary desolation of sea-wrack and coral awash in the rising tide, I caught sight of a long silver-grey shape. Then I ran forward to stare incredulously. A shark I had expected but certainly not of the type which now lay before me with the hook firmly embedded in its huge jaws.

It was Carcharodon Carcharias or, as the Australians more aptly term it, the White Death shark, one of the most ferocious killers of the deep and seldom found in the neighbourhood of land. Though the brute was not more than twelve feet long it was nearly six feet in girth and weighed 1360 lbs., while the stretch of its jaws, armed with five rows of serrated ivory teeth, was large enough to slip over my shoulders.

What an appalling mechanism of destruction it is, the ocean-going shark. This creature consisted of nothing more than a cavernous jaw and skull fastened to a backbone, a large stomach, a tiny heart and six feet of liver. Its eye was so small that it looked like Death peeping through a keyhole.

The following day was spent in completing the autopsy, and then the elated villagers bore off the slabs of flesh to their respective cooking-pots.

Man-eating sharks are generally local in their swims and from the time that we rid the channel of this ferocious specimen, the strip of water where the deaths had occurred was shark-free. Considering the circumstantial evidence coupled with the known characteristics of this particular type of shark, I have no doubt whatever that we got the actual killer.

Some mornings later I was watching the black and white crows busily cleaning up the jaws of the White Death shark on the battlements of the ruined courtyard when I was joined by a bearded ancient who might have just arrived in a cayuck from the Stone Age.

For a while, we smoked in silence, then:

"A bad one," he said, nodding at the great jaws grinning above.

"Yes. I'm afraid that there's nothing dangerous left in the channel except what may pass through by accident."

"There's another still. Smaller, different, but he's dangerous, Bwana, he's dangerous."

I sat up.

"What's that you say? There's another shark living in the channel?"

"No, Bwana. A big Chewa (jew-fish)."

"Perfectly harmless!"

"The *green* Chewa, Bwana."

"Ah! Well, I can do nothing unless you stir your lazy limbs and get me bait."

The old villain sighed, grinned and settling himself comfortably where he could inhale the full stink of the shark, contemplated his own navel.

CHAPTER 18

A GIPSY OF THE SEA

I began to notice that the light-hearted Ali was wont after dark to restrict his movements more and more to the immediate vicinity of the hut. At first I put this down to the local superstitions about the ruined Boma whose gaunt black shape took on a solidity against the night sky as though at any moment lights would stream from all the windows and voices within converse on recent leaves and the joys of the Unter den Linden.

"If you would prefer to move your sleeping mat into the Boma, Ali..."

"Never, Sah," he replied quickly. "It would be as bad as sleep on the shore."

"What's wrong with the shore? I've noticed that you've been a bit jumpy recently."

"Sah, the other night I saw a Kibwengo on the sand. There are plenty of them on Chole, and on Kibondo and Juani."

"What the devil are Kibwengos?"

"It is a little ghost-man carrying a light and you see him only on the shore, a very small bent man, Sah, hunting for fish in the seaweed and coral. I saw one the other night."

"You mean that you saw me doubled up over my shark line with a torch, my lad."

"No, no, Sah. It was there, down there near the mango trees."

"H'm."

It was after midnight when I was awoken by a nervous

tapping on the piece of canvas which formed the door of our hut and caught a glimpse of the whites of Ali's eyes shining above a dim kerosene lantern.

"Come quick, Sah! Kibwengo!"

Cursing the man for a fool I hurried after him to the edge of the sand.

"There," he cried, stretching a triumphant arm into the night. "The lamp of a Kibwengo."

Far away across the water there gleamed a tiny light, apparently on the shore of Kibondo Island.

"Idiot! It's nothing more than a fisherman inspecting his traps at low tide."

"No fisherman, Sah," replied Ali in a hoarse whisper. "The men do not go out at night to their nets in this part. See, there is a second light. Two Kibwengos!"

I focused my night glasses and for a while watched the twin points of light waxing and waning far off on the dark line of Kibondo.

"Fishermen, Ali! Good night."

"Kibwengos, Sah! Good night."

Next morning I had a word with the Jumbi of Chole.

"Do your men or the men of Kibondo go to their fish traps at night, as I have seen elsewhere?" I asked.

"No, Bwana, not at night. On the other side towards Kinasi there is a trap which is worked by night, but nowhere else."

"Surely your men use the fishing torches?"

"Never, Bwana," came the uncompromising reply.

"Last night I saw two lights over there on the shore of Kibondo," I said idly.

For a moment he looked at me with a queer inscrutable smile on his ancient face, then without further comment than a low salaam he shuffled off among the palm trees.

It was after this that I began the pernicious habit of strolling out to the shore every night in the late hours 'to inspect the view' and sure enough the tiny lights were always there; sometimes far off along the Chole sand, sometimes on the shores of the other islands. That I knew them to be the lights of fishermen detracted not an iota from the eeriness of the scene, that infinite darkness of land and sea pierced only by those queer blobs of light which legend would have as the lamps of the ghost dwarfs searching for fish in the blackness of the seaweeds. But the spectral quality of the hours of darkness on Chole Island was intensified beyond words by a purely natural phenomenon which was tenfold more sinister than the alleged Kibwengos.

The expanse of sand, perfectly smooth in daylight, would erupt after nightfall into a vast concourse of sharply pointed hillocks over a foot in height and flanked by tunnel mouths from each of which there arose a noise powerful enough to be audible at a distance of fifty yards. The whole shore-line, pinnacled like a lunar landscape in miniature, was one great purr as though all the cats in creation were asleep beneath the coral sand. The authors of this most eerie racket were burrowing crabs, nocturnal creatures of spider-like velocity and periscope eyes which twitched and waggled protestingly at the end of their stalks whenever the beam of my torch swept across them. With every fall of the tide, these crabs sprang to their duty with the energy of non-union workers, carting large loads of sand out of their burrows by balancing the mounds on their claws. Nor would they cease their labours save for an occasional fight when, standing on their high back legs and locking claws, they swirled and spun together as though engaged in some demoniacal waltz. By dawn they, their holes and their mounds had always vanished, leaving the whole surface of the shore as smooth and glistening as a bed of newly fallen snow.

The 20th century African, with his schools and Welfare and Unions, remains exactly what he was, a superstition-riddled primitive. A good example was to be found in the most intelligent member of my own crew, a man who spoke English, French, Arabic and Swahili, read considerably and was exceptionally quick in the uptake. But, just as soon as adversity touched him, the veneer of 'civilization' cracked wide open. When he felt ill in Chole Island — for that matter, all of us were ill from the same causes, insects and coralburn — he accepted our medical treatment in a spirit of courtesy and then rushed to the local Witch Doctor. Two days later I noticed that his hand was enormously swollen and, on closer examination, found that the third finger was gripped by a massive ring of some clear, yellow substance. It was so tight that the flesh stood up in ridges.

"What is this?" I asked.

The man looked at the sky and the sea and the sand at his feet.

"The Wise One gave it to me," he replied at last.

I couldn't resist it.

"Well, let me know when your finger drops off," I said carelessly.

But I had misjudged my man. His belief was stronger than his fear and the vice-like ring remained where it was until the Witch Doctor himself demanded it back. This little incident, multiplied a million-fold, is symptomatic of the basic outlook among even the better educated Africans, and the pernicious modern trend to instil in the minds of such people a kind of ersatz equality towards the white population of East Africa is doing more to disrupt and destroy not only the fundamental values but the future of a great continent than any threat from Communism. The Fabian policy of the Colonial Office, rooted in a profound ignorance of African native mentality, by undermining the white man's essential authority and discipline on the one hand while on the other flooding the country with the semi-illiterate employees of grandiose but catastrophic Colonial Development schemes, has done nothing to help Africa and everything to assist the plans of Empire-conscious India. In the communal centres of East Africa the Black, while still preserving all the superstitions and primitive reactions of his ancestors, has changed from a simple fun-loving instinctively obedient and, as such, valuable unit of a continent, into a cocky bemused and thoroughly truculent 'nigger'. But it is not his fault. It is the fault of those who, via the channels of government, dictate racial policy to the white population, and utterly disrupt the fundamental values and outlook of the black by the introduction of such calamities as Trade Unionism amid a basically primitive people. Socialist Colonial policy, by blurring the focus between the white and the black, has immeasurably strengthened the power-grip of India's expansion into East Africa. Nor must we be deceived by the fact that the majority of the swarming thousands of India's first spearhead appear to be dirty, slipshod fellows with no other purpose in life than to money-grub and breed children. Many of the first colonisers of the British Empire were little better. While the Colonial Office in London busily undermines the power of the moderate, justice-loving white man over the black primitive, the Indians are forging an unbreakable grip upon the commerce and finance of the country. At the same time their higher educated brethren are concentrating upon obtaining majority controls in the town councils of every East African community from great centres like Nairobi and Dar-es-Salaam to forgotten pimples such as Kilwa Masoko. Once these majorities are obtained, and already many have been, pressure will be brought to bear, a pressure backed by all the power of council votes and transcendant commercial teamwork, for a change in the Immigration Laws. And the shortsighted policy of the London interferers, by vitiating the authority of the white settlers, has made it certain that that change will come about. India's second spearhead will carry a very different type into Africa. It will be composed of the professional classes, lawyers, doctors, bankers, experts on minerals, farming, modern architecture, and finally, emigrating military officers. In the ranks of these men will rise India's future government in what was once British East Africa. Unless the white settlers divorce their great country from the yoke of the Colonial Office and the disruptive effects of Socialist policy among the primitive swarms of Africa, and set up an entirely separate government of their own as free from outside interference as the Australian or Canadian Parliaments, unless such measures are implemented they will lose their Continent. And they will have deserved to lose it.

Supplies were running short and we made an uneventful journey back to Mafia to revictual. And yet, is uneventful the right term when a trifling incident turns out to be the first signpost pointing the way into the future? In the little anchorage we found an errant dhow which had arrived from Muscat with a load of tiles, rugs and dried shark hides. There it lay, its rigging and forward raking masts transformed by the dying sun into cobwebs of the palest gold, a high-sterned swan-necked vision that had come drifting silently out of the centuries to drop its anchor in the bay of a forgotten isle. Spiritually it was blood perfumed with ambergris.

I had thrown overboard an old sun helmet on reaching our

anchorage, and as the longboat from the dhow drove into the shore, the captain came swaggering up the beach with my old hat hanging by its strap from his arm. He was a hawk-featured bearded Arab, his face framed in long greasy lovelocks that, escaping from a scarlet turban, fell to his shoulders in a wild profusion through which glinted and jangled a pair of golden earrings.

There was something about the fellow's cool, instantaneous possession of my former headgear which jarred upon me and, as he lounged past, drawing my sheath knife I cut the strap and caught the hat before it reached the ground. The Arab was round like a flash, his hand sliding into the open bosom of his shirt and for a long moment we eyed each other. Then with a glitter of magnificent teeth he broke into a smile and politely gave me greeting. After that, there was only one thing to be done. An Arab-speaking member of my crew brought coffee while the Rover and I sat together under the shade of the Copal trees in the fullness of that camaraderie which belongs to all who sail the ocean in little ships. He spoke shortly of the long, hazardous journey that had brought him and his medieval vessel across two thousand miles of open sea, and at great length on the iniquity of Customs and the suspicious nature of Customs officials in general. When, in answer to his questions, I told him of our expedition, he burst into such a torrent of words that it took the watchful Ali all his time to interpret.

"Sharks! Great fish!" he cried. "You must leave at once, tomorrow, for Muscat and the Gulf of Oman. *There* are the great sharks, such sharks as no white man has seen. Eight, ten or fifteen a day you will kill."

"So you think you know about sharks," I smiled.

"I should. I deal in their hides and oil," he replied hotly. I determined to test the fellow.

- 175 -

"What types do you get?" I demanded.

With a wealth of accurate detail he described in turn the Tiger shark, the White, Hammerhead, Mako and Blue Pointer, then added a close description of a dusky-coloured brute greatly feared for its cunning as well as ferocity, which tallied with no species of shark that I had ever encountered. The man was a master in his subject.

"If I go to Oman, will you join me?" I asked.

He burst out laughing.

"In that?" he cried, pointing to the *Gloria Scott*. "Why, she is not much more than thirty feet long! Many of the Oman sharks are twenty-five feet, some thirty, and because they attack when wounded it is madness to fish for them in boats smaller than fifty feet with a crew of six seamen at the very least."

"Don't be deceived by her size, my friend. She's strong enough for any shark."

"May Allah prove you right," he replied, "but I must tell you that it is terribly hot on the Oman coast and the sea not very kind to little ships. It is possible only from Ocober to March. No white man has fished those waters," he added.

"Then I shall come, but next year."

"You mean this? Good..." he nodded vigorous approval — "Allah have you in his keeping. If you want big maneaters, then you will be happy. Now, take down in your language the names of these places — Taka, Merbat, Ghubet Fazaiya — if Allah wills it, we shall meet again. You have good guns?"

"To use on sharks?"

A smile flitted across his face.

"To use on men," he said.

"You mean piracy and slavers. Then they really do exist in these waters?"

He shrugged expressively.

"Big dhows do not like little dhows when they are far from the coast," he remarked.

"What's a slave worth?" I shot at him.

"Eight thousand shillings in the inland markets... er... that is to say, Sahib... so I have heard."

"Well, my friend, since I was a little boy I have had a secret lust to shoot a slaver. I shall be off your coast next year and if any of your pirate friends come snooping around my ship they'll get a hot reception. I would prefer to fight dirty with a slaver — soft nosed bullets, like these in my belt." I waved a couple of dum-dums under his hawk beak. "Take a good look at these and at my ship and warn them to keep clear."

"Probably they will never even worry you," he grinned.

I felt my temper rising and it was all I could do not to drag him down by his earrings. There was something cold-bloodedly evil in the man.

"Maybe we'll worry *them*," I growled. "Now, goodbye, and a safe journey back."

He rose to his feet and bowed gravely.

"Allah have you in his keeping," he said.

Then, with another low salaam he sauntered away and a moment later I heard his voice raised in a screeching argument with the Indian Customs clerk. Thoughtfully I made my way back to the *Gloria Scott*.

CHAPTER 19

RED WATER

While in Mafia we added Mahommet Ali, a local fisherman, to the crew. This fellow, a lithe humanised version of a black panther, had a very narrow escape from death just prior to joining the *Gloria Scott*.

In company with seven other men, all friends and relatives, he was fishing from a light dhow between Niorora Island and the northern point of Mafia, when suddenly there appeared above the surface the great dorsal fin of a Tiger shark, heading at top speed towards the boat. The horrified men could see clearly the huge square head and barrel-shaped body approaching like a torpedo and a moment later, with a white flash of its belly, the fish rolled and smote the dhow with its great tail. In vain the crew shouted and beat the water with their long paddles as again and again, with increasing fury and recklessness, the ravenous creature repeated its charge. Water poured over the gunnels, and then came the final blow of that vast twenty-five foot projectile.

The dhow tipped, rolled and then slowly capsized, hurling men and gear into the sea as the dorsal of the Tiger shark submerged beneath them. A short half-mile separated the struggling crew from the safety of Niorora but only four of the poor devils reached it, swimming for their lives through a spume of water reddened with the blood of their four companions. The shark fed well that morning. On the following day the survivors were picked up by another dhow which fortunately came within hailing distance of the island, but as they passed near the spot where their boat had been overturned they were petrified by the reappearance of the same great dorsal fin moving in slow questing circles. It was well for them that the brute was too glutted for the moment to launch a second attack upon a boat, and slowly, lazily the awful shape turned away in search of less exacting fare.

He was an inscrutable fellow, Mahommet Ali, and the sudden twitch if his nostrils and the harsh gleam in his eyes as he told his tale conveyed a sense of horror all the more forcible for the stoic control with which he suppressed his normal emotions.

There have been more inaccuracies, and dangerous inaccuracies at that, written and spoken about sharks than about any other creature of the sea. People who have been fortunate enough to encounter only Sand sharks, Grey Nurse or Shovelnose, are often inclined to refer to the Squalidae as cowardly and easily frightened by splashing on the surface or shouting under water. Such mischievous nonsense should be treated with the contempt that it deserves, for otherwise it may cost the life of the innocent believer.

From long years of practical experience of these fish, I have no hesitation in stating that when compared with the Tiger shark, White shark, Mako and Brown shark, a man-eating tiger of the land pales into insignificance. Absolutely fearless and insensible to pain, these creatures, consuming anything and everything that does not smell of decay, will gorge themselves until they vomit, and then begin the whole business all over again. Some big-game fishermen have told me that they have actually seen Tiger sharks snap up four gallon paraffin drums and rend floating crates into splintered matchwood between their six rows of teeth, while on many occasions metal canisters and drums eaten away by the strength of the digestive juices have been found in their stomachs.

Sometimes discoveries of a more sinister nature are revealed to the horrified onlookers. One shark, taken off an Australian port, had on the side of its belly a small bulge through which, on being slit open, there instantly protruded a human hand. Rings, watches, bones, all the rubble of a bloody death are found too often in the bowels of these crafty and ferocious killers. Shortly before I reached Zanzibar, a large shark was brought in and duly cut open, revealing within a bag of money and a human skull.

The Brown shark will actually stalk its prey, moving stealthily through the shallowest water, its body matching its sandy surroundings until, with a final heave of its tail, throwing concealment to the winds it hurls itself upon its victim in no more than thirty inches of water! In its attack the shark does not turn on its back as the old superstition would have us believe. Indeed, it does the exact reverse, for it is the upper jaw that rises, so that the whole head rears up into a dreadful clown's cap above a yawning orifice bristling with bone-shearing teeth. These teeth, differing in every species, are composed of the finest ivory in the world, ivory better than that of the elephant and walrus, and they are so laid in the jaw that, when the mouth is closed, the five rear lines disappear beneath a bed of satin-soft membrane.

It is almost contradictory in creatures of such berserk ferocity that the shark should be a model parent. Yet such is the case, for not only do the young remain with the female until they are well able to care for themselves, but in certain species, on the approach of peril the female shark will open her great jaws and allow her offspring to take shelter in a compartment of her body until the danger is passed. When a female shark, incidentally always larger and fiercer than the male, is hooked and dragged up a ship's side, it is no uncommon sight to see the young, accompanied by the Pilot fish, continue to leap in the air in their efforts to follow the rapidly vanishing matron.

A female shark on the hunt represents the passage of a small community through the water. For all its bulk the great creature glides past with the lightness of a shadow, its jaws slowly opening and closing, while the little catlike eyes search the depth for prey. Before her, a herald of approaching majesty, swims the Pilot fish in its livery of gold and blue stripes, while the grey Sucker fish cling like tatters of flesh to the monster's sides and belly; behind her follow the young sharks, tearing and fighting for the guts and bits of fish flesh which spew from each fresh victim caught in the awful jaws twenty feet ahead. Brainless, merciless and insatiable, it is a procession of executioners gliding through the twilight of the sea.

Every species of shark has its own idiosyncrasies as, for example, the stealth of the Brown shark which we have already mentioned. In the case of the Tiger shark, we find a physical peculiarity which is unique to itself. Operating through a slit above each eye, a large white disc descends and ascends over the optic, and very difficult it is to decide its exact purpose. As Nature however, has an excellent reason for everything, we must look to the habits of this killer and here, in my modest opinion, we have the answer. From types of crustacea found in its stomach, it is known that the Tiger shark goes to the staggering depth of 600 fathoms and more in search of its food, and in my view these curious discs are used for the purpose of protecting the eyes from deepwater pressure. The shark would in effect hunt blind beyond a certain depth, no handicap whatever to a creature which at all times relies on its sense of smell in preference to its eyesight. When sufficiently hungry both the Tiger and the White shark will attack small boats, rending large pieces out of the gunnels in their efforts to reach their prey, and it can be safely stated that, where survivors of ships have spent a considerable time floating in tropical waters and escaped to tell the tale — a circumstance which has given rise to absurd theories as to the non-violent disposition of sharks — the fact of the matter is that there were none of the man-eating species in that locality at that particular time.

The white man is in greatest danger of all owing to the colour of his skin and for the same reason I have found that sheets of white paper thrown on the surface of the sea will quickly attract the curiosity of these predatory fish.

A shark is always hungry to a greater or lesser degree and even big crocodiles, which quite commonly swim several miles out to sea from the river mouths, are looked upon as gifts of manna and eagerly snapped up. Whatever else he is, the shark is not a coward and, with the exception of the Grampus, there is no creature that has less cause to be one. But these mighty engines of destruction have their scourges. Sea lice infest their bodies and it is no rare spectacle to behold a shark leap ten or fifteen feet into the air in a maddened effort to shake the crawling vermin from its body. Sclerosis of the spinal bone is often to be found, especially in the case of confirmed man-eaters who prefer the leisurely killing of bathers and canoe-men to the more vigorous efforts necessary for the pursuit of fish schools; and finally, on the principle of Jack and the Giant killer, the jovial little Porcupine fish means death by perforation for the shark which swallows it.

Lazily dangerous by nature, the faintest smell of blood will rouse the shark into such a homicidal frenzy that it will wriggle up the shore on its belly until it is almost out of the water, or jump high above the sea with jaws snapping and clashing in its efforts to reach its prey.

But it is at night that they are at their most dangerous, cruising through the dark waters with redoubled vigour while a wake of phosphorescent fire bubbles and flickers behind the beat of the great pectoral fins.

When I am fishing for Marlin, Sailfish or any of the great Game-fish I am conscious of a sneaking feeling that unless my opponent is really required for food or shapes like a record fish, I shall let him go after the fight is over. There is no pleasure to be found in killing the innocent under guise of sport. It is for that reason that I prefer shark fishing, for it is a battle *à l'out-rance* with one of the few creatures in Nature which generates active hatred in the breast of man.

The tropic dawn was turning the sea into a lake of fire when we headed south for our base camp on Chole. Though the 14-foot tide would be changing from flood to ebb over the nigger-head corals there should be time to make our way safely through the dangerous tricky straights separating Mafia from Kibondo Island.

Ah, shades of Ghilani! We had rounded Point Kisimani, the southernmost tip of Mafia, and the coconut palms of Kibondo were already on our starboard quarter when it occurred to me that we were bearing at a very strange angle. In reply to my questions the Nahoda was emphatic. He knew his job; let the Bwana M'kouba continue to catch fish.

A few minutes later, there came a yell from for'ard and dashing to the side I glared down at a sight which brought my heart into my mouth. Hardly awash in water of the palest jade green instead of blue, a huge mass of Brain coral slid past within three feet of the ship's side. And we were still moving at 4 knots! I shouted below to stop the engine and, at that very moment with all the roguery of Fate, there came a screech from my reel and I was into a big fish! I had left the rod in a stern socket and as I rushed towards it I could see the powerful cane bending like a whip. It was no time for niceties, with the ship in fearful danger of having her whole bottom ripped out by the first coral head in our path. Slamming on the brake to its tightest, I put my feet against the taffrail and heaved. The fish tore for the boat in a savage burst of speed that left two hundred yards of slack floating in the water and from these tactics I knew him for what he was, a huge barracouda. Nothing mattered now but to take up the slack before his next charge. I wound in madly and then all in an instant my fingers froze on the reel handle.

From beneath the stern there streamed a great cloud of sand like the dust trail of a motor car passing over a desert. The keel was grounding in the bottom of the sea. Though the engine had stopped we were still proceeding under momentum, and abandoning both rod and barracouda I ran for the bows, shouting at the crew to fling the anchor overside. Fortunately, Anna had beaten me to it and under her cool directions the terrified Ali had hurled the anchor into the water where a white mist of sand showed that the flukes were already gripping.

There was not a moment to lose. The tide was dropping swiftly and, grounded already, it was only a matter of minutes before the ship would roll over on her side unless we were able to mount the legs in time. Anna and I staggered across the deck with the heavy timbers while Ali and the Nahoda, plunging overside into the water, tried to tear away the bolthole covers. But a fool had painted them over.

"Rip off the blasted things with your knife," I yelled to Ali, as a slight tremor shook the vessel.

There was a short blasphemous struggle followed by a groan of relief. The legs were in place with mighty few minutes to spare. Now, at last, we had a chance to survey the general situation.

The barracouda had fought himself free, leaving a vile mess of line drifting on the surface. A mile distant on the port side a ribbon of blue marked the channel from which we had deviated under the expert captaincy of our precious Mafia Nahoda, while all around us lay a pale green translucence glimmering with coral and sand ripples over which the tide was falling so rapidly that, on clambering down the side a few minutes later, we found ourselves in little more than three feet of water. And there we stayed, perched on that accursed plateau amid the bristling niggerheads for six solid hours. I confess that I was deeply worried for, with a congenital idiot as a Nahoda, how the deuce were we going to find our way off again and back to deep water on the rising tide without ripping out the ship's guts on the coral spires? Any deviation from the channel even at high tide was an invitation to disaster and as we were now separated from that channel by a mile of water, it seemed that our only chance was to attract the attention of a fishing canoe which lay between us and our objective. If, when the tide rose to its highest, the fisherman was to proceed as pilot a short distance in front of our bows, then we should make it safely.

Our united shouts having failed to reach him, a succession of revolver shots worked so admirably that in one convulsive movement the distant figure sprang to his feet and seizing a paddle set off in the opposite direction as though the devil himself was grasping for the tail of his canoe. By now, our nerves were so ragged that we sent a couple of shots after him to speed him on his way and then settled down to wait.

Through the glasses we could see on the horizon a long low

smudge which was the Tanganyika coast and the delta of the
Rufiji river. Originally we had planned to make our way up
that maze of yellow forest-girt waters winding away into
the very heart of Africa, but the condition of the *Gloria
Scott's* hull had become so doubtful, thanks to reefs and sand-
banks and torn planking, that it seemed very unlikely that we
could now fulfil that part of our project. This was a very serious blow, for the area of the Rufiji, in addition to the many
forms of game living in its bushland and the hippos and exceptionally large crocodiles that swarm along its banks, is the scene
of a present-day drama in the best tradition of adventure stor-
ies. Last year £ 60,000 worth of elephant tusks, the spoil of a
gang of ivory poachers, was smuggled out of the Rufiji in the
holds of dhows bound for Muscat. The bushland, far up the
tributaries of the great river, conceals the headquarters of a
highly-organised gang of desperadoes engaged in wholesale
ivory poaching. The gang is composed of Arabs, half-breeds
and negroes, and led by one who is as gifted in his generalship
as he is ruthless in his methods. This man, a kind of Moriarty
of the ivory poaching world, is a full-blooded African negro
and his evil record fully justifies the high price which has been
placed on his head. Game scout after game scout have stalked
the gang through the hinterland of the Rufiji. Few have returned alive to tell the tale. When first I heard the story from
the coast natives, I was inclined to dismiss it as gossip until
every word was confirmed to me by the Game Warden of a
neighbouring district. Later I received further confirmation
from the lips of one whose name is legendary along the whole
coast of Tanganyika, an extraordinary character known as the
King of the Rufiji who, claiming descent from the Phoenicians
and worth more than a million pounds sterling, yet prefers to
live surrounded by his feudal retainers on a little fever-ridden

island than waste his declining years in chasing the luxuries of the civilised world. And there are those who believe that adventure and the bizarre no longer exist!

At the end of three hours, the ship had taken in so much water through her strained seams that we had to work the bilge pumps, repeating the process at short intervals until, lifting at last on the rising tide, and having allowed two more hours to drag by, the engine was started and slowly, nervously, we commenced that never-to-be-forgotten mile.

Anna was on the harpoon deck to give warning of any coral heads immediately in our path while I worked the sounding lead, and Ali relayed our messages in Swahili to the Nahoda at the wheel. Down in the engine room Klein and the new hand baled like madmen to keep the water below the fly-wheel bearing level, using five gallon drums which were faster than the bilge pump. At times we had only eighteen inches of clearance between our keel and the coral tops but, thanks to Anna's signals out there on the harpoon platform, we were able to zigzag our way around the appalling masses of coral which every now and then loomed up at us through the clear jade of the water. Our hearts seemed to cease beating on more than one occasion as huge crags passed directly beneath the ship, but the tide was now rising rapidly and what a short time before would have spelt our doom now scraped under us by inches. At long, long last, or so it appeared to the tight-lipped men and woman on the *Gloria Scott,* the bristling coral heads glimmered in a deeper green, became diffused into a medley of shadows and then sank abruptly into the wonderful transparent blue of the deep channel. The ship was safely through!

The fireflies were already winking among the palm trees when, two hours later, the anchor splashed down in the darkening waters of Chole bay. Wearily we dragged ourselves up the beach and fell on to our camp beds. To eat would be too much effort, to light a candle torment by inches. It was good just to lie still in the darkness and watch the stars blazing above in the purple eternity of heaven.

Usually the winds quietened down in the evening and then was the signal for our sufferings to begin. My God, those nights! It was as though the single word 'meat' flashed from antennae to antennae, and the attack was on. Sausage flies, flying ants and Praying Mantii, Chole versions of our Kilwa visitors, we came to regard as old friends, good fellows, gentlemen and sportsmen for, though they might flow down our throats with every gulp of tea or entangle themselves in our hair, they did not venture upon our very life blood. But, oh, the others! Black mosquitoes fell upon us in clouds, so that every calm night meant thickened and swollen limbs. But even worse were the sand-flies, those minute specks possessing the biggest bite relative to their size of any creatures in the world. They clustered on our bodies like grains of sand, and bit and bit and bit. Accidentally our mosquito nets had been left behind in Kilindoni and so despite the damp heat we were reduced to wrapping ourselves to the chin in towels like mummies and enveloping our faces in butterfly nets. Yet even so it was impossible to close an eye before the dawn brought relief.

Nevertheless, Nature supplied us with some unexpected allies to whom we shall be indebted so long as memory prevails. From every crack and crevice came the lizards until there would be ten, twenty, fifty of the jolly fellows rushing up and down the walls and eating, chewing, gulping the winged demons which were eating, chewing and gulping us. Heaven reward the lizards!

I shall use our nocturnal torments on Chole as an opportunity to say a word about Anna, a word which is very much overdue. We all suffered, even my tough Africans, but she, a delicately skinned woman, suffered naturally much worse than anybody else. The courage of woman is so far above the masculine as to be almost beyond our comprehension. All her life, Anna had been devoted to an exceptional degree to those arts and tittivations which play, and rightly play, an important part in the existence of every chic female. Clothes, cosmetics, perfumes, the creative charms of the Paris salons, such had been the métier which she shared in common with every other smart and soignée woman of the world. Yet, throughout the whole of this expedition, she bore every form of hardship and suffering without a complaint or whimper. She did all the camp cooking, save for the crew, preserved all specimens by smoking and salting, doctored us all, including the crew, to the fury of the local Witch Doctors, and being very susceptible was scarred and bitten throughout her face and limbs by those accursed insects in a way that was pitiable to see. I urged her again and again to return to Morocco until I had completed my exploration of the Mafia waters, and received always the same firm reply — "Never, until you have finished your work. You would all starve without me or forget your anti-fever pills or something stupid like that." What can one say in the face of this kind of thing?

But even at the worst we created some happiness in the midst of torment by simply lighting the lamp in our crazy shack and drinking cold tea while, eating coconuts with one hand and slapping sandflies with the other, we gossiped about Paris and our memories. And ever and always, out in the black waters, my lines lay in wait for the maw of any killer which might pass our way, while the legend of the big Jewfish recurring often to our minds encouraged us to continue in the face of all discomforts.

CHAPTER 20

PAUSE IN ADVENTURE

Bait was still our pressing difficulty and I was driven to wandering for miles, often up to my thighs in swamp and stagnant water, in search of wild pig. The winds varying almost daily in the birth pangs of the monsoon had killed the local fishing and little or nothing was to be caught in the waters of the bay, while the Kinasi was impossible of approach. Driven almost to desperation, I did a dreadful thing. I shot a white Egret. Fortunately I killed it instantly but I must confess that I felt a murderer as I regarded the body of the lovely fragile bird with its delicate lace-like feathers and beautifully chiselled long black beak and legs. It seemed as though one fished for the Devil with a bait of Venetian glass. But the great Chewa, if it really existed, I had to get. And then...

We were attacking a mess of bully beef by the light of a candle when the most fearful racket arose from outside the hut where an empty petrol tin acting as an alarm was now clanging its way around the bole of a palm tree. We rushed forth and falling upon the rope hauled with all our strength while Anna ran for the rifle. We could feel a considerable weight at the far end but the pull of a fish in deep water is so misleading that it is almost impossible to judge with any certainty the probable size of one's opponent. We heaved back, and the line ripped through our fingers.

"Drop it!" I shouted a warning.

There was a howl and a string of curses as the rope burnt the skin from our hands. The fish tore away towards the Kin-

THE GREEN CHEWA

HEAD OF 80 LB. CAVALLI JACK WITH SEIZED REEL

DHOW IN MOONLIGHT

DAWN OVER CHOLE ISLAND: KINASI PASS IN BACKGROUND

asi Pass as we fumbled and fell over each other in our efforts to hold him. After a desperate struggle we recovered a few yards and then again the line ripped through our grasp like a red-hot wire. Far out in the darkness of the mid-channel came a sound of splashes and plunges as some heavy body broke surface. The taut line swerved in a great arch and we hauled as one man.

"Another Pa Pa," gasped Ali.

"Hell knows! Pull and keep pulling."

For a while we made little impression and then there came a slow, sullen 'give' in the line.

"We win, Sah!"

"We won't, if you don't keep heaving," I panted back.

At last, with the greater part of the line on shore, I was able to run down to the water's edge and pass my torch beam slowly over the stygian blackness.

Nothing...nothing... yes, something now, something which threw back a reflection from the light.

It was nothing else than a huge yawning *mouth* coming slowly towards me across the smooth dark surface of the sea. Was it a shark? Then: — "Pull, boys, pull for all you're worth," I yelled. "It's the giant Jewfish!"

Heaving and straining we managed to drag the fish into the shallows but not a yard further, for the strength of the ugly misshapen thing was so formidable that with its fins spread upon the coral it was able successfully to resist our united efforts. The vast jaws and the phosphorescent quality of its eyes flashed back the torch light. I made my way warily towards it until I could see the deep green sheen which showed it belonged to that rare variety of Jewfish which will, and does, attack man. It is the big relation of the Groper, itself a sulky fish which possesses the pleasant habit of biting off the hands of divers.

Seizing a steel pickaxe I smote it three blows on the skull with every ounce of my strength. The jaws merely yawned up at me like an open grave, and it was not until I shot it with my revolver that the great body relaxed amid the weeds and coral spires.

It was really an enormous specimen, over 6 ft. 4 inches in length with a girth of 4 ft. 7 inches and a span around the jaws of 3 ft. 6 inches. The comparatively light weight, only 230 lbs. lay in the fact that at least one third of the whole creature consisted of its huge cavernous mouth bristling with row after row of needle teeth. As I contemplated this horrific fish with its heavy undershot jaw and general resemblance to a predatory but discontented financier, my conscience smote me again that I should have killed the delicate loveliness of the egret to have brought up this hideousness from the depth of the sea. That the bait had worked, it seemed to me, was an insufficient excuse.

The Jewfish remains in many ways a creature of mystery in spite of the fact that it is found in most tropic seas. Its type of habitat and feeding are well known but the size to which these fish may run is a matter of conjecture. The official World Record is 550 lbs., yet serious and experienced fishermen have claimed on good testimony to have encountered Jewfish of at least 2,000 lbs. in weight within thirty miles of Mombasa harbour. The predatory habits of these hunchbacked terrors of the coral grottoes remain a large and sinister question mark, but there is a growing school of thought that inclines to the theory that a proportion of the deaths ascribed to sharks and barracouda belong in fact to Jewfish. To my certain knowledge, on two occasions white men were attacked by Jewfish during the time of our expedition in East African waters. One of these men, a District Officer, was swimming to the bathing raft in

Lindi harbour when he became aware of a shadow rising slowly beneath him. Fortunately, he was only a few yards from the raft and, hurling himself forward at top speed, pulled himself over the edge. As he did so, he heard from immediately behind him a sound like the clash of a closing trap and peering down from the safety of the raft he was horrified to see a huge green Jewfish sinking back gradually into the depth.

There is strong evidence that this type of fish employs the suction of its gigantic mouth as a means for 'inhaling' its prey.

There have been many cases of sudden *quiet* disappearances of bathers in tropical waters, disappearances lacking entirely in the cries, screams and excessive discharge of blood that characterise attack by shark and barracouda. My friend, Mr. Arnold Klosser of Zanzibar, was an actual witness of a suction death committed by a Jewfish in Lamu. A twelve year old Arab boy was swimming from a dhow when the dark shape of a Jewfish rose suddenly from the depth and halting about two feet below the boy's body opened its great jaws. The poor lad disappeared like a bit of fluff into a carpet cleaner, while a series of tiny whirlpools momentarily disturbed the surface. Though people rushed to the spot and beat the water with poles and paddles, the body vanished as though engulfed in a moving tomb.

The prowess and ferocity of the Jewfish, especially of the green variety, deserve a great deal more attention than they have as yet received from both icthyologists and big game fishermen.

The weather was becoming steadily worse, and more than once we had to turn back from the Kinasi Pass without even reaching it. Grave looks were exchanged between our crew and the local natives and these took shape finally in a warning from the Jumbi which simply boiled down to this — "The

Kinasi is now impossible. For the next four months if you are caught by the Acusi (south-west monsoon) out there in your little boat, it will be very dangerous. If your engine stops, it will mean death. Leave it."

It dawned fine and we made one last attempt. But as we drove between those towers of coral, following the precarious zig-zag route necessary if we were to avoid ripping out our keel on the submarine spires beneath, we were caught up in the gigantic swell of the Indian Ocean, staggering, rolling, dipping, while the table crashed over and the forty gallon water tanks slid about the deck and thundered against the railings.

Clinging on for dear life, we trolled from the stern. Crash! Anna's line was ripped off, the ship rolled, there came a great swirl far behind our stern and the fish had broken the line. Again, the same thing but this time the 6 inch spoon had been bitten clean in two! Then again, and the heavy game line was torn to shreds. It was utterly impossible to fight these giants under such conditions, to battle with fish which could snap a 90 lb. test line capable of holding 200 lbs. or bite through a metal spoon, while we tried to hang on to our rods and at the same time keep our balance on a deck heaving, reeling and dipping in the face of a white-capped mountainous swell which threw us about like the proverbial cork. There was nothing to be done but return to base.

That evening as the sun went down through a wrack of storm clouds, I did some thinking.

We were a crew of wrecks. Six months had passed since we had tasted meat or fresh vegetables save for an occasional potato. None of us, not even my hardy Africans, could walk properly owing to the continual friction of fine coral sand on continuously wet feet, so that we all hobbled like a flock of ducks. We were scarred and swollen with insect bites, and sleepless nights had raised the nervous tension of one and all almost to breaking point. Though fortunately the others had so far escaped, I was racked with malaria. Our little ship the *Gloria Scott,* twice aground on coral reefs and once on the actual shore, was leaking badly through her seams and taking in water through her deck planks. And yet, in despite of these physical evils, was there not another and more lasting side? Had not this life of free adventure already taught us truths so deep and abiding that they shone like stars within our poor earthly minds? There on the coral beach with the sound of the wind ruffling the palm leaves overhead, I knew in my heart that the magic had entered into our blood, wedding us to the lure of the tropic seas until death do us part. The things that are taken for granted, ordinary every-day things such as regular meals, entertainments, doctors round the corner, dependence on others, had become redundancies divorced from reality. In exchange we had discovered discomforts, even dangers but, above all, the great and the little freedoms. Even our physical senses of sight and hearing and smell had become markedly more acute. The loneliness of life in the wild places is the loneliness of a peace beyond expression. Money is less important than safety pins. The break of a clear dawn promising a good run of fish or the fact that a certain wild pineapple should be ripe before evening are matters of far greater moment than the utterances of wrangling politicians or the latest impositions of our economic masters. The cloth skirt shields you from nakedness; if hungry, there lies an oyster on the reef or a stafeli on a tree branch. Knowing hardship, often afraid, sometimes in pain, you are a Free man. You are God under a blue sky.

I knocked out my pipe, took a last look at the Kinasi crags black and stark against the glory of the afterglow and went in to Anna. She was sitting on her camp bed, cleaning the sand out of Jum-Jum's eyes and surrounded by the usual haze of mosquitos.

"The expedition is over," I said abruptly. "There is nothing more that we can do in these waters; anyway for at least six months."

She put Jum-Jum from her lap.

"I've expected that you would tell me this for some days past," she replied. "And you've made the right decision. It's no use closing our eyes to the fact that the monsoon is here, and after the Kinasi I feel somehow that the smaller fish in the Mafia channel, sheltered as it is, would mean little or nothing to you."

"I hate to be beaten like this, because of an accursed storm season," I frowned.

"You've not been beaten," she said. "Instead you've had far more success than you deserve or I ever hoped for. You have caught one World Record, the only world record fish held in the whole Continent of Africa; you've broken the 80 lb. test line record; and rid Chole of a man-eating shark not to mention that green horror the other night. Then we've got the films of that incredible palace on Songa Manara, and all our reef work in addition to the many types of fish which we have caught and photographed and recorded. The time has surely come."

We stared at each other for a long moment across the smoky kerosene lamp.

"We'll go back to Morocco for a while just to recuperate," I said, "Mind you, we've learnt a great deal and made a lot of mistakes which will not be repeated on the next Expedition. Next time..."

"You intend to come back — here?"

"Never. My dear girl, there are not enough big fish in these

African waters, though I still believe that the Mafia shelf may have a secret or two down in its depth. No, not back here but to the Red Sea and Muscat, to the place where I saw three Hammerhead sharks, two Manta rays and a Dorado Dolphin all within eyeshot at the same moment! Of course, it is only possible to fish there for three months in the year in a small boat but, good God, the place is teeming with enormous shark and yet has never been attempted with modern big-game tackle. But in addition to shark fishing I want to try something which, so far as I am aware, has never been attempted. I want to make an expedition at the bottom of the sea!"

She stared at me aghast. "My God," she cried, "are you now suggesting that we should sell up our home and invest in a bathysphere?"

"No, no, of course not. But if I encase our movie cameras in a watertight transparent box with exterior controls, use a glass mask and light oxygene tanks and smear myself plentifully with anti-shark ointment..."

"Does it work?"

"To the best of my belief, admirably. Now, if we were to make a safari along the coral reefs of the Arabian Sea at a depth of 25 feet, the water is sufficiently deep for the larger sharks and Manta ray while the light is strong enough for perfect visibility. Think of it, Anna! We could actually stalk these creatures through their own incredible landscape of shapes and colours, through the great empty cathedrals of the sea. Here are possibilities without end."

"I can see one end very clearly." She looked at me thoughtfully. "Granting that it might be possible from the point of equipment, when do you propose that we should come up again?"

"Every few hours. But there is no question of 'we'. I want

- 197 -

you up top. I must have somebody on whom I can rely completely to make sure that the schooner follows me mile by mile.
We would sleep on board and devote every other day to shark
fishing on the surface. But the main thing would be to make an
expedition of several months' duration along the bottom of the
sea. Give me a crew of tough Arabians on the ship and..."

I caught her eye and fell silent.

"Will you ever find what you are looking for?" she asked as
though speaking to herself.

"Not in this world. But I must go on looking just the same.
It's damnably hard on you."

She went to the door and I could see her figure in her boyish
shorts and shirt outlined against the evening sky. Far above,
two dark specks flew to the Northward over the palm forests
of Mafia, now shrouded in the fast-gathering darkness.

When she spoke again there was a catch in her voice.

"There they go, wild duck or herons or something, our sym-
bol flying North."

"The way to Muscat," I answered.

"The way to... weariness, perhaps, and heat and danger
and all the things, as a woman, I hate. And yet, the wandering
way to freedom, perhaps fulfilment. I must have three months
to get well again in my body and nerves and then, if you want
us, I and Jum-Jum will come with you."

Her hand found mine in the gloom of the hut.

INDEX

- 202 -